GRAMMAR
STEP-BY-STEP

VOLUME 2

GRAMMAR
STEP-BY-STEP

Lorraine Nichols Pratt

National Textbook Company
a division of NTC/CONTEMPORARY PUBLISHING GROUP
Lincolnwood, Illinois USA

ISBN: 0-8442-5493-2

Published by National Textbook Company,
a division of NTC/Contemporary Publishing Group, Inc.,
4255 West Touhy Avenue,
Lincolnwood (Chicago), Illinois 60646-1975 U.S.A.
9 RD 9 8 7 6

CONTENTS

GRAMMAR

STEP-BY-STEP

UNIT 1

The Simple Sentence

UNIT I

The Simple Sentence

SKILL 1

Identifying Linking Verbs and Their Modifiers

The ability to recognize a verb is the first and most fundamental skill required for an understanding of the structure of an English sentence.

The second most essential skill is the ability to identify the verb as either *linking* or *action.*

Linking verbs constitute the smaller of the two verb groups. A list follows of the eleven principal linking verbs and the various forms of each. The recognition of linking verbs in any of their forms is a necessary skill and one that can best be ensured through memorization.

Linking verbs should be marked with the abbreviation LV.

		am	was	be
B E		are	were	been
		is		being

SENSES VERBS

Look	looks	looked	looking
Smell	smells	smelled	smelling
Taste	tastes	tasted	tasting
Sound	sounds	sounded	sounding
Feel	feels	felt	feeling

"GRABS"

Grow	grows	grew	growing	grown
Remain	remains	remained	remaining	
Appear	appears	appeared	appearing	
Become	becomes	became	becoming	
Seem	seems	seemed	seeming	

A

Without referring to the list on the preceding page, write the linking verbs and their forms on a separate sheet of paper in the same order and arrangement.

B

Number your paper from 1 to 15.
Write the linking verb in each sentence after the corresponding number.
Underline each and place the letters **LV** above it.

1. One of the dogs is very ferocious.

2. The sea breeze was extremely refreshing.

3. The hikers appeared weary by early afternoon.

4. The noises in the attic sound ominous to me.

5. The answer to the riddle remains a mystery.

6. The cherry pies tasted rather sour.

7. During the political rally the child grew bored.

8. After football practice I am always exhausted.

9. The problem of pollution becomes more serious.

10. The young woman's manners were appalling.

11. The results of the tests seem conclusive.

12. The peanut butter smelled rancid to me.

13. Mrs. Ginsberg seemed satisfied with Ruth's progress.

14. Leonard's solution to the problem was impractical.

15. Vicki becomes dizzy in high places.

Ominous means having a menacing or threatening aspect.

If something is *appalling*, it is disgusting or horrifying.

Auxiliary verbs should be marked with the abbreviation *aux*.

An *auxiliary verb* sometimes precedes a linking verb. Note the words circled below.

aux   LV   aux   LV
(is) being   (should) seem

The following verbs are auxiliary verbs.

can	shall	will
could	should	would

has	may	do
had	must	did
have	might	does

Be (all forms)

am	was	be
are	were	been
is		being

A *linking verb phrase* consists of a linking verb <u>preceded</u> by one or more <u>auxiliary</u> verbs. Each group of words below is a linking verb phrase.

aux LV
<u>can feel</u>

aux   aux LV
<u>must have felt</u>

aux   aux   aux   LV
<u>could have been feeling</u>

The forms of the verb **BE** are used both as <u>linking</u> and <u>auxiliary</u> verbs. Note below.

LV
David (is) my brother.

aux LV
David (is) <u>looking</u> tired.

A

■ Without referring to the list, write the auxiliary verbs on a separate sheet of paper in the same order and arrangement.

B

■ Number your paper from 1 to 12.

■ Write the linking verb or verb phrase in each sentence beside the corresponding number.

■ Underline each and place **LV** above the linking verbs and **aux** above auxiliary verbs.

1. Norma's reply might have appeared abrupt to some.

2. The vote of the committee must be unanimous.

3. The author's identity would have remained a secret.

4. The entire meal tasted delicious.

5. Then he could feel certain of the results.

6. Julio may have been the sender of the flowers.

7. The baby had been growing restless during the performance.

8. The students were more attentive after their vacation.

9. I am being optimistic about the weather.

10. Nancy's views sound too radical to the group.

11. Rodney should have become an actor.

12. The problems on the test did seem difficult.

Sometimes an *adverb* will separate the auxiliary verb from the linking verb. Note the word circled below.

The letters *adv* are used as the abbreviation for *adverbs*.

The boy <u>has been</u> cooperative.
     aux LV

The boy <u>has</u> (always) <u>been</u> cooperative.
     aux   adv   LV

An adverb can precede a simple linking verb. Note below.

         adv   LV
She (eventually) became the owner.

Adverbs indicate *when, how,* or *to what extent* a situation exists. Study the examples below.

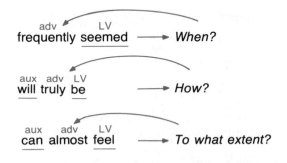

  adv   LV
frequently seemed ⟶ *When?*

aux adv LV
will truly be   ⟶ *How?*

aux   adv   LV
can almost feel ⟶ *To what extent?*

The adverb *not* can be contracted with a simple linking verb or with the auxiliary verb in a linking verb phrase.

 LV adv   LV adv
He is not here.   ⟶ He is n't here.

    aux adv LV   aux adv LV
She has not been well. ⟶ She has n't been well.

Here are some adverbs that tell *when.*	Here are some adverbs that tell *how* and *to what extent.*
always	actually
eventually	almost
never	also
now	definitely
often	gradually
recently	only
sometimes	probably
soon	really

A

■ On a separate sheet after the corresponding number, write the linking verb or verb phrase and any adverbs in the order in which they appear.

■ Underline the verb or verb phrase, and label each word on your paper appropriately.

EXAMPLE: Her casserole has never tasted bland.

aux   adv   LV
has never tasted

1. The mother has sometimes seemed partial to her oldest son.

2. The bride suddenly appeared ill.

3. The pies smell done.

4. Father had not been looking healthy.

5. The venture has almost been disastrous.

6. The committee wasn't favorable to our request.

7. The humidity will probably remain high.

8. The hot bread always smells delicious.

9. He grew despondent after his wife's death.

10. The food hasn't been tasting right.

B

■ On a separate sheet after the corresponding number, write the linking verb or verb phrase and any adverbs in the order in which they appear.

■ Label each word on your paper appropriately.

1. The other Smiths aren't our relatives.

2. The followers had soon become disillusioned.

3. Carla often seemed preoccupied.

4. My assistant is busy with another client.

5. The author couldn't have been he.

6. The accident had really been unavoidable.

7. The patient's hair quickly became grey.

8. Her desire for a good education grew stronger.

9. I did not feel qualified for the job.

10. The butler's story had also sounded shaky.

SKILL TEST

■ On a separate sheet after the corresponding number, write the linking verb or verb phrase and any adverbs in the order in which they appear.

■ Label each word on your paper appropriately.

1. The team had often seemed discouraged.

2. The men were afraid of the lizard.

3. Dolores can really be a nuisance at times.

4. The rose bush has also been looking better.

5. Julia eventually became my wife.

6. The yogurt doesn't taste the same.

7. The neighbor's children have always been considerate.

8. You must never sound irritated with the customers.

9. Who would have been the best?

10. To our investors the project still looks unsafe.

SKILL 2

Identifying Prepositional Phrases

The letter *p* is used as the abbreviation for the word *preposition.*

Prepositions are a group of words that indicate relationship. See the underlined words below.

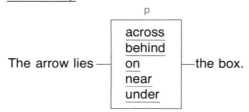

The arrow lies ——— the box.

Each time the preposition in the sentence above is changed, the relationship between the arrow and the box also changes.

The following are prepositions. Memorization best insures their recognition.

aboard	below	for	through
about	beneath	from	throughout
above			
	beside	in	to
across	besides	into	toward
after			
	between	like	under
against	beyond	near	underneath
along			until
	but	of	up
amid	by	off	upon
among			
	concerning	on	with
around		over	within
at	down		without
	during	past	
before		since	
behind	except		

A

■ Study the prepositions listed. Then without referring to the list, write them on a separate sheet of paper in the same order and arrangement.

B

■ On a separate sheet after the corresponding number, write the prepositions that you find in each sentence.
■ You should find 45.

1. Our children skate on Lake Ontario for several months during the winter.

2. Like many other students I put too little time into my studies.

3. All of the officers live within walking distance except Officer Bauer.

4. After her death the rose was found pressed between the pages of her diary.

5. To his amazement across the table sat his grandmother whom he had not seen since his boyhood in Buenos Aires.

6. The mail carrier comes past our house during the afternoon.

7. Above the door of the cabin hung the notice pinned to the board by the local sheriff.

8. She could tell us nothing about our son and directed us down the hall to another doctor.

Tenacity means courage, determination, and mental strength.

9. At first she fought against heavy odds; however, through her tenacity she somehow rose above the obstacles.

10. Amid the shouts of the mob, the sheriff stood with his deputy in silent defiance.

11. Before dawn the troops began their march along the river several miles below the bridge.

12. Until the day when other energy sources are developed, we should do without pleasures that involve the use of much gasoline.

13. Around midnight the clock mysteriously fell off the wall and made a noise that was heard throughout the house.

14. Beside the lake and along the trail were footprints that led toward the shack behind the bunkhouse.

Objects of prepositions should be marked with the abbreviation *OP*.

The letter *n* is used for the abbreviation for the word *noun*.

A *prepositional phrase* begins with a preposition and ends with an object of the preposition. The object of the preposition answers the question *what* or *whom* when asked <u>after</u> the preposition.

what? ↓
p   n(OP)
(to school)

whom? ↓
n(OP)
(for the child)

Objects of prepositions can be *nouns* —names given to <u>people</u> (girl, students, pilot, Americans) and <u>things</u> (New York, page, engines, desert, birds). Note the examples above.

The letters *ob pro* are used as an abbreviation for *object pronouns*.

Object pronouns can also be objects of prepositions. The following are object pronouns:

Singular	to me to you to her, him, it, whom
Plural	to us to you to them

The abbreviation *id pro* is used to label *indefinite pronouns*.

Indefinite pronouns can be objects of prepositions. The following are indefinite pronouns:

any	anyone	anybody	anything
each	everyone	everybody	everything
none	no one	nobody	nothing
some	someone	somebody	something

few	one(s)
several	other(s)
many	another
more	either
most	neither
all	both

Demonstrative pronouns are indicated by the abbreviation *d pro.*

Demonstrative pronouns can be objects of prepositions. The following are demonstrative pronouns:

this	that	these	those

The abbreviation *itr pro* is used to indicate *interrogative pronouns.*

Interrogative pronouns can be objects of prepositions. The following are interrogative pronouns:

what	which

Reflexive pronouns are indicated by the abbreviation *r pro.*

Reflexive pronouns can be objects of prepositions. The following are reflexive pronouns:

Singular	myself yourself himself, herself, itself
Plural	ourselves yourselves themselves

A

■ Study the groups of words that can be objects of prepositions.
■ On a separate sheet of paper, list the following:

1. five nouns that refer to people and five nouns that refer to things

2. the object pronouns in the same order and arrangement as listed

3. the indefinite pronouns in the same order and arrangement as listed

4. the four demonstrative pronouns

5. the two interrogative pronouns

6. the seven reflexive pronouns

On a separate sheet of paper, number from 1 to 20.

After the corresponding number, label the part of speech of each word in the phrase.

EXAMPLE: (without pain)

(p   n(OP))

1. (by someone)
2. (without us)
3. (against himself)
4. (except Jill)
5. (between these)
6. (during what)
7. (toward this)
8. (from nothing)
9. (for herself)
10. (over whom)

11. (before most)
12. (after breakfast)
13. (to those)
14. (upon something)
15. (aboard them)
16. (across which)
17. (behind that)
18. (about others)
19. (below us)
20. (concerning it)

Words that give information about the noun or pronoun that serves as the object of the preposition are called *adjectives.* Study the examples below.

The abbreviation *adj* is used to indicate *adjectives.*

```
    p    n(OP)
( with kittens )

    p    adj ——▶ n(OP)
( with (little)  kittens )

    p    adj   adj   n(OP)
( with (cute) (little)  kittens )

    p    adj   adj    adj   n(OP)
( with (two) (cute) ,  (little)  kittens )
```

The letters *n adj* are used as the abbreviation for the words *noun adjunct.*

When <u>nouns</u> precede and modify objects of prepositions, they function as <u>adjectives</u> and are called *noun adjuncts.* Note the examples below.

p   n adj   n adj n(OP)
(during the (school) (lunch) hour)

A

■ On a separate sheet of paper, number from 1 to 5.
■ Write labels for all the words in each prepositional phrase in the order in which they appear.

EXAMPLE: (with hot chicken soup)

(p   adj n adj n(OP))

1. (about attractive, durable floor covering)

2. (through narrow mountain passes)

3. (from large school projects)

4. (on small, inexpensive camp stoves)

5. (by school tennis teams)

B

■ On a separate sheet of paper, number from 1 to 5.
■ Write labels for all the words in each prepositional phrase in the order in which they appear.

1. (with durable, accessible light switches)

2. (in desolate desert country)

3. (for late jet flights)

4. (during longer lunch periods)

5. (about new, inexpensive oil filters)

Label *conjunctions* with the abbreviation *cj.*

When *conjunctions* are used, one prepositional phrase can contain two or more objects of one preposition.

```
     p    n(OP)      cj   n(OP)
( for students  and  faculty )
```

```
                (OP)        (OP)
     p    cj   ob pro  cj   id pro
( with  both   her   and  others )
```

Adjectives can also be joined by conjunctions and conjunction pairs.

```
     p    adj   cj   adj    n(OP)
( by tired  but  happy children )
```

```
     p     cj    adj  cj   adj     n(OP)
( from  either  reel  or  rotary lawnmowers )
```

Conjunctions and conjunction pairs that connect nouns and adjectives in prepositional phrases are the following:

1. and
2. or
3. but

4. either . . . or
5. neither . . . nor
6. both . . . and
7. not only . . . but also

A

■ Study the list of conjunctions and conjunction pairs.
■ Without referring to the list, write them in the same order and arrangement on a separate sheet of paper.

B

■ On a separate sheet of paper, number from 1 to 11.
■ After the corresponding number, write the part of speech of each word in the phrase in the order in which it appears.

1. (with tart but delicious lemon pies)
2. (against that or me)
3. (down narrow streets and alleys)
4. (on large cattle ranches)
5. (by themselves)
6. (with lovely monogrammed pocket handkerchiefs)
7. (for both hard-working and innovative partners)
8. (behind neither this one nor the other)
9. (without what)
10. (concerning not only him but also us)
11. (near either Tokyo or San Juan)

C

■ On a separate sheet of paper, number from 1 to 10.
■ After the corresponding number, write the part of speech of each word in the phrase in the order in which it appears.

1. (through many sad and difficult experiences)
2. (except these and others)
3. (about either one)
4. (by neither average nor superior seniors)
5. (for which)
6. (to both you and her)
7. (around either New Orleans or St. Louis)
8. (along beautiful, sandy beaches)
9. (of city or state taxes)
10. (in ourselves and several others)

D

■ On a separate sheet write each of the sentences below.
■ Underline and label the verb or verb phrase in each; label any adverbs.
■ Place parentheses around the prepositional phrases; label all words within.

1. They are confident about complete success in both this contest and that.

2. Several of them still look fresh enough for dance decorations.

3. This one will perhaps be the last of many wonderful and exciting evenings.

4. The new general could only have grown disheartened with such frequent, unnecessary, and costly delays.

5. Within five or six short months we have been in twelve countries and twenty major cities.

6. Throughout that one long day without her, all had somehow remained optimistic except me.

7. The subject would appear too mature for young ones.

8. The objections to either dress standards or discipline rules haven't seemed too strong.

SKILL TEST

■ On a separate sheet write each of the sentences below.
■ Underline and label the verb or verb phrase in each.
■ Label any adverbs.
■ Place parentheses around prepositional phrases, and label all words within.

1. The dress with sleeves isn't attractive.

2. The sick man did sometimes feel wretched about not only these but also others.

3. The association has also been growing indifferent toward both teachers and us.

4. In view of some recent unusual and favorable forecasts, the plan now sounds feasible.

5. The news concerning either protest demonstrations or school disruptions is very upsetting to her.

SKILL 3

Identifying Noun Signals and Adverbs in Prepositional Phrases

The symbol *adj³* will help you remember these 3 special adjectives.

The adjectives **a, an,** and **the** function as *noun signals.* A noun always follows immediately or closely behind them. The question *what* asked after a noun signal indicates the noun. Study the examples below.

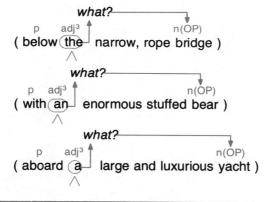

The abbreviation *ps pro* is used to indicate *possessive pronouns.*

A caret (∧) placed beneath a word indicates that it is a noun signal.

Possessive pronouns also function as noun signals. They indicate ownership of the noun(s) that follows.

Possessive pronouns are the following:

	1st person	my box
Singular	**2nd person**	your box
	3rd person	her box, his box, its box, whose box

	1st person	our box
Plural	**2nd person**	your box
	3rd person	their box

A

■ Study the list of possessive pronouns. On a separate sheet without referring to the list, write them in the same order and arrangement.

B

■ On a separate sheet of paper, number from 1 to 10.
■ After the corresponding number, write the part of speech of each word in the phrase in the order in which it appears.
■ Place a caret (∧) beneath each noun signal, and draw an arrow to the noun(s) it signals.

EXAMPLE: (from the oldest sister)

(p adj³ adj n(OP))
        ∧

1. (by your last exam day)
2. (with an unusual man and woman)
3. (before his distinguished but stern face)
4. (through not only the last crisis but also its painful aftermath)
5. (near the other)

6. (except a small and luminous nugget)

7. (without him or her)

8. (during their excellent dinner and the entertaining floorshow)

9. (to Des Moines)

10. (in our latest car design)

Use the
abbreviation
ps id pro to label
*possessive
indefinite pronouns.*

When an apostrophe *s* is added to an indefinite pronoun,
it also functions as a noun signal. It is called a *possessive
indefinite pronoun.*

p   ps id pro   n(OP)
(to everyone's surprise)

p   ps id pro n(OP)
(concerning one's future)

The letters *s ps n*
are used to indicate
a *singular
possessive noun.*

When an apostrophe *s* ('s) is added to a singular noun, it
becomes possessive and functions as a noun signal. It is
called a *possessive noun.*

p   s ps n   n(OP)
(in Jill's mind)

p   adj³   s ps n   n(OP)
(for the store's opening)

The letters *p ps n*
are used to indicate
a *plural possessive
noun.*

When an apostrophe is added to a plural noun that ends
with an *s,* it also becomes possessive and functions as a
noun signal.

p   adj³   p ps n   n adj   n(OP)
(in the students' math books)

p   adj³   p ps n   n(OP)
(near the apartments' entrance)

When a plural noun does not end in *s,* an apostrophe *s* is added to make it possessive.

p   adj³   p ps n   n(OP)
(about the children's health)

p ps pro p ps n   n(OP)
(for   my   feet's benefit)

The four kinds of noun signals are the three special adjectives (a, an, the), possessive pronouns, possessive indefinite pronouns, and possessive nouns.

A

■ On a separate sheet of paper, write five prepositional phrases using a possessive indefinite pronoun in each as a noun signal.
■ Place a caret (∧) beneath the noun signal; label all the words.

B

■ On a separate sheet of paper, change each of the following nouns into possessives by adding appropriate endings.
■ Place a noun after each.
■ Place a caret (∧) beneath each possessive noun, and label it appropriately.

1. a student___ _____
2. the car___ _____
3. my father___ _____
4. a teacher___ _____
5. the door___ _____
6. the students ___ _____
7. the cars ___ _____
8. our fathers ___ _____

9. the teachers ___ _____
10 six doors ___ _____
11. three mice ___ _____
12. his children ___ _____
13. the oxen ___ _____
14. most men ___ _____
15. ten geese ___ _____

■ What are the four kinds of noun signals? List them on your paper.

C

- On a separate sheet of paper, number 1 through 8.
- After the corresponding number, write the part of speech of each word in the phrase in the order in which it appears.
- Place a caret (∧) beneath all noun signals.

1. (within one's reason)

2. (about my frequent tardies and absences)

3. (to either's wild imagination)

4. (with an amiable and witty one)

5. (for the schools' new music program)

6. (to her club's treasurer)

7. (between those)

8. (for children's curly hair)

Adverbs in prepositional phrases <u>precede adjectives</u> and answer the question *how* about the adjectives.

$$\overbrace{\qquad}^{how\ beautiful?}$$

p   adv   adj   n(OP)
(among the very ⌊beautiful botanical gardens)

A

- On a separate sheet of paper, write the five phrases below inserting adverbs that answer the question *how* and that appropriately modify the adjectives they precede.
- Place a caret beneath all noun signals, and label all words.

1. (throughout the _____ long night)

2. (at the _____ gruesome movie)

3. (about a(n) _____ complicated person)

4. (to a(n) _____ insensitive remark)

5. (for his _____ brilliant mind)

B

■ On a separate sheet of paper, number from 1 to 10.
■ After the corresponding number, write the part of speech of each word in the order in which it appears.
■ Place a caret (∧) beneath all noun signals.

1. (on her very long hair)

2. (about that utterly ridiculous remark)

3. (with the children's friends)

4. (throughout its remarkably splendid history)

5. (past an old delapidated one)

6. (for these and us)

7. (of the candidate's almost disastrous remark)

8. (by either a very entertaining comedian or an exceptional vocalist)

9. (from himself and everyone)

10. (beyond anyone's most absurd imagination)

C

■ On a separate sheet of paper, write each of the sentences below.
■ Underline and label the verb or verb phrase in each; label any adverbs.
■ Place parentheses around the prepositional phrases, and label all words within.
■ Place carets beneath all noun signals.

1. You usually are sensitive to both her feelings and needs.

2. Ahmad shouldn't be feeling depressed about this.

3. After a little more of my sister's tutoring, I should be ready for it.

4. The counselor had always seemed patient with everyone's problem.

5. Did he often remain moody for extremely long periods?

6. This might not be the last of our accountants' errors.

7. They are confident of their success in this election or the next one.

8. The patients would only have grown more discouraged about themselves.

9. During the last years of her relatively long life, she really became disillusioned with them.

10. Father remained silent during the children's seemingly endless explanations.

SKILL TEST

■ On a separate sheet of paper, write each of the sentences below.
■ Underline and label the verb or verb phrase in each; label any adverbs.
■ Place parentheses around the prepositional phrases, and label all words within each.
■ Place carets beneath all noun signals.

1. Of the many very interesting activities at the fair, Charles would probably have been bored with most.

2. Her parents are anxious about her behavior and our discipline.

3. In others' opinions Julio has always been considerate of us.

4. Nathan hasn't been absent from either Ms. Yen's math class or my English class.

5. She sometimes was weary after the extremely arduous arguments and anxieties of the court room.

SKILL 4

Identifying Subjects of Sentences

The abbreviation *S* is used to label the *subjects* of sentences.

The *subject* of a sentence is the particular person(s) or thing(s) about which a thought is expressed or information given. It is usually a *noun*.

The subject is identified by asking the questions *who* or *what* before the verb. Note below.

His parents <u>appear</u> anxious.
             LV

Who?
          LV
          <u>appear</u>

Who?
n(S)   LV
parents <u>appear</u>

Nominative pronouns can also be subjects of sentences.
The following are nominative pronouns:

The abbreviation
n pro is used to
indicate *nominative
pronouns.*

Singular	I am you are she is, he is, it is, who is
Plural	we are you are they are

Object pronouns can <u>never</u> be used as subjects of sentences.

I
Susanne and ~~me~~ are twins.

Indefinite pronouns, demonstrative pronouns, and interrogative pronouns can also be subjects of sentences. Note below.

(S)
id pro   LV
(All) <u>are</u> his friends.

(S)
d pro   LV
(These) <u>are</u> his friends.

(S)
itr pro   LV
(Which) <u>are</u> his friends?

A

■ Study the list of nominative pronouns. Then without referring to it, write the pronouns on a separate sheet of paper in the same order and arrangement.

B

■ On a separate sheet write each of the sentences below.
■ Underline and label the verb or verb phrase in each; label any adverbs.
■ Place parentheses around prepositional phrases; label all words within.
■ Label the subject.

1. I am the last on the library list.

2. To some this tastes better with milk or cream over it.

3. The water smelled contaminated.

4. To our regret most have not been talented.

5. Of the three which is bigger?

6. For years she was the winner of every tournament.

7. One appeared confused during your presentation.

8. The chair was an antique.

Subjects can be joined by conjunctions to form <u>compound subjects</u>.

```
 cj      n(S)      cj    n(S)   LV
Both balloons (and) punch were free.
```
```
 (S)              (S)
n pro  n(S)  cj  id pro  aux     LV
She, Bob, (or) anyone can become eligible.
```

A

■ On a separate sheet of paper, number from 1 to 8.
■ After the corresponding number, write the subject(s) of each sentence and any conjunctions in the order in which they appear.
■ Label each word appropriately.

1. Either he or she has been inaccurate.

2. The men and boys will not be the contestants.

3. Both these and those are unnecessary.

4. We or anyone would probably have sounded incoherent.

5. This and more must now become the subject of our investigation.

6. Not only you but also others then became active.

7. Either Rebecca or she is the writer.

8. They don't look good.

One or more prepositional phrase can separate a subject from the verb of the sentence.

    n(S)   LV
One girl (in the show) was very talented.

  (S)
id pro   LV
Most (of the exhibits) (at the fair) were excellent.

IMPORTANT

The subject of a sentence is <u>never</u> found in a prepositional phrase.

A

 On a separate sheet of paper, write each of the sentences below.

 Underline and label the verb or verb phrase; label any adverbs.

 Place parentheses around the prepositional phrases, and label all words within each phrase.

 Label the conjunctions and subjects.

1. The filing of the application by January was imperative.

2. No one but him has been very interested.

3. She and one of the counselors will be the administrators of the test.

4. Donors of either money or food will still remain anonymous.

5. The entertainment, the exhibits, and the food at the county fair must have seemed exceptional to everyone.

When a question contains a simple linking verb, the subject usually follows the verb.

LV (S) n pro
Are (they) the sponsors?

When a question contains a linking verb phrase, the subject follows the first auxiliary verb.

aux (S) id pro aux LV
Could (anyone) have been suspicious?

A

- On a separate sheet of paper, number 1 to 5.
- After the corresponding number, write the subject(s) of the sentence and the verb or verb phrase.

1. Is the soup hot?
2. Can Sue and she be my helpers?
3. Would any of you have become disturbed?
4. Was that strange to you?
5. Are Harvey and he ready?

B

- On a separate sheet of paper, number 1 to 5.
- After the corresponding number, write the subject(s) of the sentence and the verb or verb phrase.

1. Wasn't her father our last mayor?
2. Am I the winner?
3. Did the witness at his trial seem nervous?

4. Are these and those acceptable?

5. Will you and the other lawyer on the case be ready?

A subject can be preceded by the same parts of speech that precede an object of the preposition.

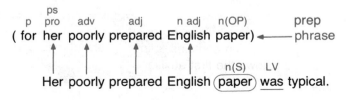

Noun signals also precede and indicate the subject of the sentence.

A

- On a separate sheet of paper, write each of the sentences below.
- Underline and label the verb or verb phrase; label any adverbs.
- Place parentheses around the prepositional phrases, and label all words within each phrase.
- Label the subjects and all words that precede them.

1. In any business an intelligent and honest worker is a great asset.

2. Your offer of our much needed financial assistance seems generous.

3. The tall buildings and majestic spires of New York City truly are impressive.

4. The extremely hot summer months had finally grown unbearable.

5. For the trip a small, inexpensive stove like that one would have been sufficient for the campers' needs.

6. Student discipline at Lillian Graycloud's school has definitely become a problem.

B

■ On a separate sheet of paper, beside the corresponding number, write the subjects and verb or verb phrase of each sentence, choosing the correct pronoun.
■ Label the words on your paper.

1. Theresa and **me** / **I** aren't sisters.

2. Both **them** / **they** and **him** / **he** seem ready.

3. That group or **we** / **us** would be better.

4. Either **us** / **we** or **her** / **she** was the problem.

C

■ On a separate sheet of paper, write each of the sentences below.
■ Underline and label the verb or verb phrase; label any adverbs.
■ Place parentheses around the prepositional phrases, and label all words within each phrase.
■ Label subjects and all words that precede them.

1. The guitar music at the concert in the park sounded great.

2. Another's child always appears better behaved.

3. Neither these nor our city's needy should ever become objects of anyone's pity.

4. A really sharp girl would have felt insulted by their remarks.

5. Which of these is the expensive one.

6. In the morning I always feel grouchy.

7. Some birds' diseases can be fatal to children.

8. Many in their group are dependent on themselves for support.

SKILL TEST

■ On a separate sheet of paper, write each of the sentences below.
■ Underline and label the verb or verb phrase; label any adverbs.
■ Place parentheses around the prepositional phrases, and label all words within each phrase.
■ Label subjects and all words that precede them.

1. Our country's flag remains a symbol of freedom and justice.

2. For everybody the old but beautiful homes along the river near New Orleans still are a big attraction.

3. Anyone's slightly insensitive remark would become a reason for hysteria.

4. These gruesome horror movies are harmful to your very small children.

5. She might be a detriment to herself.

SKILL 5

Identifying Linking Verb Complements

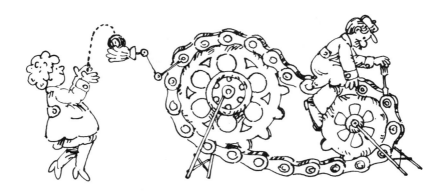

The letters *PN* are used to indicate a *predicate nominative*.

A sentence with a linking verb and a subject also contains a third basic element called a *complement*. A complement <u>completes</u> a sentence.

A noun that follows a linking verb and <u>completes</u> the sentence is called a *predicate nominative.*

```
n(S)  LV adj      n(PN)
```
John <u>is</u> a loyal (friend) (of mine).

A predicate nominative <u>renames</u> the subject. It can be exchanged with the subject without changing the meaning of the sentence.

```
      n(S)    LV        n(PN)
```
The winner <u>was</u> an American.

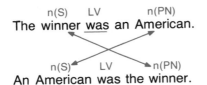

```
      n(S)     LV      n(PN)
```
An American <u>was</u> the winner.

Nouns used as predicate nominatives are often preceded by noun signals. The predicate nominative can be easily determined by asking the question *what* after the noun signal.

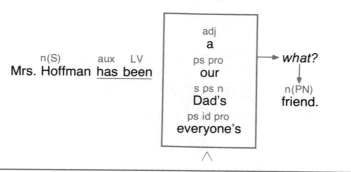

$$\begin{array}{ccc}
\text{n(S)} & \text{aux} & \text{LV} \\
\text{Mrs. Hoffman} & \underline{\text{has been}} &
\end{array}$$

adj
a

ps pro
our

s ps n
Dad's

ps id pro
everyone's

→ *what?*

n(PN)
friend.

A

- On a separate sheet of paper, write each of the sentences below.
- Underline the verb or verb phrase.
- Place parentheses around prepositional phrases.
- Label all words in the sentence.
- Indicate that the subject and predicate nominative rename each other by writing an equation after each sentence.

EXAMPLE:

ps pro n(S) LV adj n(PN) p id pro(OP)   (S)   (PN)
Your brother <u>is</u> a help (to everyone).   brother = help

1. Elizabeth could be the reader in our skit.

2. Education should definitely be your goal.

3. She remained Carl's friend after the separation.

4. One is the winner's trophy.

5. I am now a grandmother.

6. That should have been everyone's choice.

7. Either Bob or Vince is today's quarterback.

8. Retreat would never be her answer.

9. Ms. Seidletz had recently been their guest speaker.

10. Charlie is an inspiration to us.

The same parts of speech that precede objects of prepositions and subjects (adjectives, noun adjuncts, adverbs, conjunctions) also precede predicate nominatives.

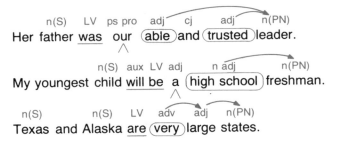

■ On a separate sheet of paper, write each of the sentences below.
■ Underline the verb or verb phrase.
■ Place parentheses around the prepositional phrases.
■ Label all words in the sentence.

1. Some of these are the very poorest examples.

2. Most now are a very loyal and conscientious group of employees.

3. That has become my sister's most cherished experience.

4. The book was a humorous and delightful collection of stories.

5. The quite strange and very creative originator of the idea wasn't a member of anyone's project team.

Sometimes no noun signal follows the verb to indicate the predicate nominative. The predicate nominative can still be easily determined by mentally inserting a noun signal after the verb.

the what?

(S)
n pro   LV
They were attractive and vivacious cheerleaders.   n(PN)

A

■ On a separate sheet of paper, write each of the sentences below.
■ Underline the verb or verb phrase.
■ Place parentheses around the prepositional phrases.
■ Insert the noun signal **the** after the verb followed by the question **what;** label the predicate nominative.
■ Label all other words in the sentence.

1. These students will be regular contestants in the games.

2. Two were very accomplished violinists.

3. Many senators in Washington are experienced and expert lawyers.

4. He and she have become Olympic gold medal winners.

5. None became America's largest and wealthiest shareholders.

6. Several in the group were honor students.

7. Some tourists have become competent photographers.

Nominative pronouns serve not only as subjects of sentences but also as predicate nominatives. As predicate nominatives they rename the subject.

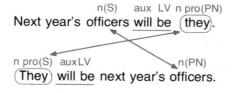

```
                n(S)    aux  LV  n pro(PN)
Next year's officers will be  (they).
```

```
n pro(S)  auxLV
(They) will be next year's officers.
           n(PN)
```

IMPORTANT

Object pronouns should <u>never</u> follow linking verbs as predicate nominatives.

```
                        LV   ob pro
The last ( on the list ) was  me.
```

The last (on the list) was I.

On a separate sheet of paper, write each of the sentences below, choosing the correct pronoun.

Underline the verb or verb phrase.

Label all words in the sentence.

1. You are **whom** / **who?**

2. The club's last winner of the award was **her** / **she.**

3. The last one won't be **me** / **I.**

4. The best could never be **us** / **we.**

5. The district champions will probably be **they** / **them.**

Indefinite, demonstrative, and reflexive pronouns can also serve as predicate nominatives.

$$\text{The advantages } \underset{LV}{\underline{were}} \text{ } \overset{\overset{(PN)}{\text{id pro}}}{\text{(many)}}.$$

$$\text{Their conclusions } \underset{LV}{\underline{are}} \text{ } \overset{\overset{(PN)}{\text{d pro}}}{\text{(these)}}.$$

$$\text{His enemy } \underset{LV}{\underline{is}} \text{ } \overset{\overset{(PN)}{\text{r pro}}}{\text{(himself)}}.$$

Predicate nominatives can be compound.

<pre>
        n(S)   aux   LV   n(PN)   cj   n(PN)
The refreshments could be (doughnuts) and (cider).
</pre>

A

■ On a separate sheet of paper, write each of the sentences below.
■ Underline the verb or verb phrase.
■ Place parentheses around the prepositional phrases.
■ Label all words in the sentence.

1. Her excellently executed sketch was one of many contributions.

2. Their best specimens are those.

3. Either Rodney or Calvin might possibly be he.

4. Marcia's best judge was herself.

5. Each truly is the other's most faithful friend.

6. They are very good baseball coaches.

7. With little effort she could become an actress, a surgeon, or anything.

8. Both's final questions should be these and others.

9. He was who?

10. The winners were neither.

Adjectives can also function as linking verb complements. Such adjectives are called *predicate adjectives*. A predicate adjective, unlike a regular adjective, does not precede a noun. Instead it modifies the subject of the sentence.

<pre>
                    n(S)   LV   P Adj
The entertainer's dress was gorgeous.
</pre>

The abbreviation *P Adj* is used to indicate a *predicate adjective*.

The complement is a predicate adjective if a noun signal cannot precede it.

the → ✕

n(S)   LV   P Adj
These blouses seem expensive.

The complement is a predicate adjective if the words *people* or *thing* can be mentally inserted after it.

n(S)   LV   P Adj
His decision was dangerous. ◄ *(things)*

n(S)   LV   P Adj
George seems tired. ◄ *(people)*

A

■ On a separate sheet of paper, write each of the sentences below.
■ Underline the verb or verb phrase.
■ Test for predicate adjectives by inserting the word **people** or **things** after the complement. (Watch for predicate nominatives.)
■ Label all words in the sentence.

1. She would not have been untruthful.

2. Everyone's children usually are loud on such occasions.

3. A fall from that height would surely be fatal.

4. One of the instructors was the originator of this very excellent plan.

5. The discipline seemed necessary, appropriate, and adequate.

6. Others have become very prominent doctors, lawyers, and diplomats.

7. The people in Huxley's society would be neither handicapped nor needy.

8. She is now being cooperative toward the other committee members.

9. He or I should be the one for the job.

The letters *P Adv* are used to indicate a *predicate adverb*.

Adverbs also serve as linking verb complements. They answer the questions *when* and *where* when asked after the linking verb. Adverbs that serve as linking verb complements are called *predicate adverbs.*

A single word, two words, or a prepositional phrase can serve as a predicate adverb.

when?

```
        n(S)   LV     P Adv
The  test  was  (yesterday).
```

when?

```
        n(S)   LV     P Adv
The  party  was  (last night).
```

when?

```
        n(S)  aux  LV         P Adv
The  play  will  be  (( on Wednesday afternoon )).
```

where?

```
  n pro(S)  LV  P Adv
    It    is  (here).
```

where?

```
  n pro(S)   LV          P Adv
    It     was  (( at Mrs. Shen's house )).
```

A

■ On a separate sheet of paper, write each of the sentences below.
■ Underline the verb or verb phrase.
■ Place parentheses around the prepositional phrases.
■ Label all words in the sentence.
■ After each sentence write the question that the complement answers.

1. The end will be soon.

2. The auditions might be next week.

3. Her boss was at the convention.

4. The geometry test will be tomorrow morning.

5. The enemy is near.

6. The duel had been before dawn.

B

■ On a separate sheet of paper, write each of the sentences below.
■ Underline the verb or verb phrase.
■ Place parentheses around the prepositional phrases.
■ Label all words in the sentence.

1. Everyone's guests can't be here for the same show.

2. One of the teachers has become hard and impersonal.

3. Mrs. Hudson's son now remains our single benefactor.

4. Both reviews and exams are next week.

5. Those in the rear will be we.

1. A stockholder should feel very satisfied with this explanation.

2. The winner is he or I.

3. Some of the final contests were last night.

4. That was in the vault.

5. The department's new aide will be someone from your office.

1. Mr. Lopez and his wife are here.

2. None of them are new courses.

3. The worst of them might be those and these.

4. The culprit was himself.

5. The woman's answers were wrong.

■ On a separate sheet write the sentences below, choosing the correct pronoun.
■ Underline the verb or verb phrase.
■ Place parentheses around prepositional phrases.
■ Label all words in the sentences.

1. The latest member of our committee was **he** / **him.**

2. It has sometimes been not only **they** / **them** but also **us** / **we.**

3. The last one was neither **her** / **she** nor **me** / **I.**

1. Carlos and **her** / **she** often appeared indifferent.

2. **Who** / **Whom** sounded worse?

3. My sister and **I** / **me** have always been healthy.

1. To Vince and **I** / **me** the error seemed deliberate.

2. The prizes for Rebecca and **them** / **they** are cameras.

3. Her partner is the woman with your neighbor and **he** / **him.**

SKILL TEST

■ On a separate sheet of paper, write each of the sentences below.
■ Underline the verb or verb phrase.
■ Place parentheses around the prepositional phrases.
■ Label all words in the sentence.

1. These often appeared very playful and docile.

2. The last performance was last night.

3. To her, Edith's fresh-baked cookies really smelled delicious.

4. Each has now become one of our most loyal supporters.

5. I am somebody in a hurry.

6. The wild boars are quite large and very fierce.

7. She is in her office.

8. The one in charge is he in the blue suit.

SKILL 6

Identifying Action Verbs and Their Modifiers

The letters *AV* are used to indicate an *action verb.*

Action verbs are a large group of verbs that express the doing of something. They can express either physical or mental action.

AV	AV
These <u>eat</u> anything.	My secretary <u>expects</u> a raise.

The action verb in a sentence can be located by using the following methods:

a. Watch for verb endings.
attack<u>s</u>, attacke<u>d</u>, attack<u>ing</u>

b. Look for them after auxiliary verbs.
   aux   AV
We ⟨have⟩ <u>driven</u> to Tuscon several times.
   aux aux   AV
She ⟨had been⟩ <u>swimming</u> that morning.

c. Ask the questions *do what, does what,* or *did what.*

did what? ⟶
      AV
His best friend <u>told</u> him the good news.

■ Number your paper from 1 to 10.
■ Write the action verb or verb phrase in each sentence beside the corresponding number.
■ Underline each and label appropriately.

1. To our surprise he returned in the afternoon.
2. These among others doubted during the difficult time.

3. My wife will call for her around noon.

4. The wealthy old gentleman had driven here in his Cadillac.

5. Everything happens to me.

6. After the referee's signal they crept toward each other.

7. The downtown streets glistened in the evening mist.

8. Before everyone's eyes she fell to the floor.

9. Both the young children and adolescents are attending on Saturday night.

10. Both of them have sold to some of the very best schools.

Adverbs can tell *how, when,* and *where* the action of the verb is done. These questions must be asked after the verb or verb phrase. Adverbs that answer these questions are said to <u>modify</u> the verb.

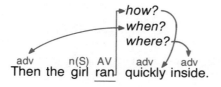

how?
when?
where?

adv   n(S)   AV   adv   adv
Then the girl ran quickly inside.

When prepositions are not followed by objects of prepositions, they usually function as adverbs.

how?

AV   adv
The horse rolled over.

Two words can function as a single adverb.

when?

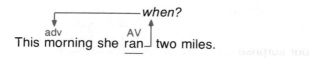

adv   AV
This morning she ran two miles.

Some adverbs modify other adverbs. Such adverbs can be identified by asking *how* before other adverbs.

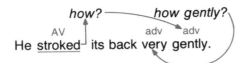

how? ———— *how gently?*

AV   adv   adv
He <u>stroked</u> its back very gently.

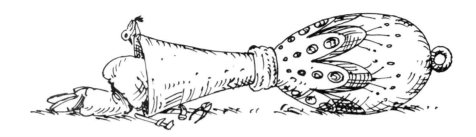

A

- On a separate sheet of paper, write each of the sentences below.
- Underline the verb or verb phrase.
- Write the adverb questions above each verb, and draw an arrow to each adverb.
- Label all words in the sentence.

1. Yesterday she had diligently searched everywhere.
2. The streets were mysteriously deserted that day.
3. The puppy whined so pitifully last night.
4. Then the sirens blew very loudly.
5. He will probably visit here tomorrow morning.

1. Outside the leaves were gracefully swirling around.
2. Later the officials and their guests were temporarily allowed aboard.
3. Yesterday morning we reluctantly went there.
4. Her agent has proceeded very cautiously lately.
5. Who will be here this morning?

Conjunctions can connect two or more action verbs. Verbs connected by conjunctions are called *compound verbs.*

Verbs that form a compound verb usually have similar endings. They express the same time (or tense) and are said to *parallel.* Parts of a compound verb should always parallel.

$$\underset{\text{AV}}{\text{Gail sings}}\ \underset{\text{cj}}{\text{(and)}}\ \underset{\text{AV}}{\text{dances.}}$$

$$\underset{\text{AV}}{\text{He rose}}\ \underset{\text{cj}}{\text{(and)}}\ \underset{\text{AV}}{\text{ran}}\ \text{from the room.}$$

One auxiliary verb can assist two or more verbs that are parallel.

$$\text{She}\ \underset{\text{aux}}{\text{(had)}}\ \underset{\text{AV}}{\text{fought}}\ \text{and}\ \underset{\text{AV}}{\text{lost.}}$$

Two or more auxiliary verbs can assist a single action verb.

$$\text{Ted}\ \underset{\text{aux}}{\text{(can)}},\ \underset{\text{aux}}{\text{(should)}},\ \text{and}\ \underset{\text{aux}}{\text{(must)}}\ \underset{\text{AV}}{\text{fight.}}$$

A

■ On a separate sheet of paper, write each of the sentences below.
■ Underline the verbs or verb phrases.
■ Place parentheses around the prepositional phrases.
■ Label all words in the sentence.

1. Suddenly another fainted and fell over.

2. All afternoon the newly hired wood finisher had been cleaning, varnishing, and polishing.

3. This was bought yesterday but has been returned today.

4. They were and are going with us.

5. Dad has hoped, worked, and saved for years.

6. The patient still cried, kicked, or threatened.

B

■ On a separate sheet of paper, write each of the sentences below.
■ Underline the verbs or verb phrases.
■ Place parentheses around the prepositional phrases.
■ Label all words in the sentence. (Watch for linking verbs.)

1. That night we sat, talked, and reminisced for most of the evening.

2. Hopefully my greedy relatives shall never know.

3. Either her semi-final or final judging is today.

4. Everyone's parents would so strongly object to it now.

5. Surely an efficient auditor can begin and finish here in two hours.

6. The auditor's mistake in the preparation of this would have been a disastrous event.

7. You may yet win in the final competition this afternoon.

8. It has been broken but will be repaired.

SKILL TEST

■ On a separate sheet write each of the sentences below.
■ Underline the verbs or verb phrases.
■ Place parentheses around the prepositional phrases.
■ Label all words in the sentence. (Watch for linking verbs.)

1. That night the angry and frustrated gorilla roared loudly and beat violently upon the cage's bars.

2. Recently the somewhat controversial review was published in Chicago.

3. In everybody's opinion those with the slightest hesitation should not have been allowed in.

4. Neither this nor that could ever be the choice.

5. A few have been fully developed but are not being produced now.

SKILL 7

Identifying Action Verb Complements

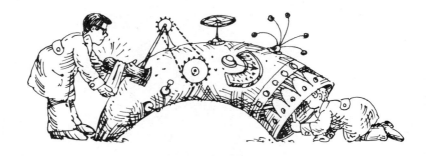

The letters *DO* are used to indicate a *direct object*.

Sometimes an action verb is followed by a complement, the name of a person or thing toward which the action of the verb is directed. Such a complement is called a *direct object*.

A direct object can be easily located by asking *whom* or *what* after the action verb.

$$\text{what?}$$
$$\text{AV(t)} \qquad \text{n(DO)}$$
My secretary <u>mails</u> the letters.

$$\text{whom?}$$
$$\text{aux} \quad \text{AV(t)} \quad \text{n(DO)}$$
I <u>have invited</u> Althea.

The letter *(t)* over a verb indicates that it is *transitive*.

An action verb that is followed by a complement is said to be *transitive* because the action of the verb can be <u>transferred</u> to a direct object.

A direct object can be compound.

$$\text{whom?}$$
$$\text{n(S)} \quad \text{AV(t)} \quad \text{n(DO)} \quad \text{ob pro(DO)}$$
The manager <u>fired</u> the cook and him.

Direct objects can be nouns, object pronouns*, indefinite pronouns, demonstrative pronouns, reflexive pronouns, and interrogative pronouns. Note below.

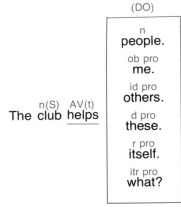

(DO)

n
people.

ob pro
me.

id pro
others.

n(S)   AV(t)
The club helps

d pro
these.

r pro
itself.

itr pro
what?

*Nominative pronouns are <u>never</u> used as direct objects. They never follow action verbs.

Some action verbs are never followed by direct objects. The action cannot be transferred to a receiver (direct object). Such verbs are said to be *intransitive*.

The letter (i) over a verb indicates that it is intransitive.

what?

n pro(S)   AV(i)
He   often complained (about the food).

A

■ Number your paper from 1 to 20.
■ Ask the proper questions after each verb below, and decide if it is transitive or intransitive.

1. disappear	**6.** flourish	**11.** object	**16.** furnish
2. laugh	**7.** discover	**12.** complete	**17.** sit
3. solve	**8.** ignore	**13.** dismiss	**18.** rise
4. occur	**9.** arrive	**14.** fall	**19.** bring
5. hold	**10.** avoid	**15.** sleep	**20.** chuckled

B

■ On a separate sheet write each of the sentences below.
■ Underline the verb or verb phrase.
■ Place parentheses around the prepositional phrases.
■ Label all words in the sentence.
■ Designate action verbs as transitive or intransitive.

1. The guests laughed.
2. You tell great jokes.
3. The judge chose several.
4. We cheated ourselves.
5. Others delayed and lost.

6. This convinced me.
7. Somebody hid these.
8. Both came and brought gifts.
9. Iris sleeps on the top bunk.
10. I objected to the decision.

C

■ On a separate sheet write each of the sentences below.
■ Underline the verb or verb phrase.
■ Place parentheses around the prepositional phrases.
■ Label all words in the sentence.
■ Designate action verbs as transitive or intransitive. (Watch for linking verbs.)

1. Contestants must not consult any of these.
2. Bonnie's grandfather won and lost several fortunes.
3. The boys arrived at the camp before us.
4. The athlete even surprised himself this afternoon.
5. One of these is the problem.
6. The owner or manager will exchange them.
7. The accident occurred around noon.
8. Those are very tasty.
9. She ruined her guitar and is buying another.
10. The luggage is on board.
11. Howard really liked spinach but hated turnips.
12. Mrs. Ortega hadn't heard about the proposal.
13. Kimberly seldom complained about the service.

■ On a separate sheet write each of the sentences below.
■ Underline the verb or verb phrase.
■ Place parentheses around prepositional phrases.
■ Label all words in the sentence.
■ Designate action verbs as transitive or intransitive.

1. Some advertisements are false and definitely illegal.

2. The stranger waved at me and drove on.

3. The boys jumped the ditch and injured themselves.

4. Some were overseas during the war.

5. Then the owner or manager will exchange these.

6. Have you burned the dinner again?

7. Anyone could beat me at tennis.

8. This is a gift from my mother.

9. Beth must change to another train in St. Louis.

10. The news shocked not only her but also others.

11. The results were announced at noon.

An *indirect object* is a noun or pronoun that indirectly receives the action of the verb. It answers the following questions:

to ⟨ what? whom?   for ⟨ what? whom?

The abbreviation IO is used to indicate indirect objects.

Indirect objects always precede direct objects in sentences.

what?──────────┐
                           ↓
AV(t)   n(IO)   n(DO)
The pitcher threw the (shortstop) the ball.
                        └─ *to whom?* ◄─┘

52

Note the various kinds of indirect objects.

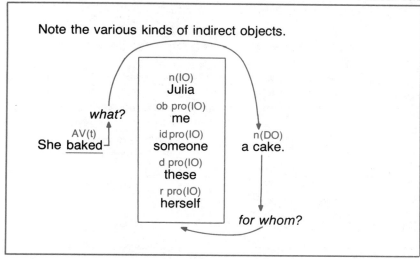

Indirect objects can be compound.

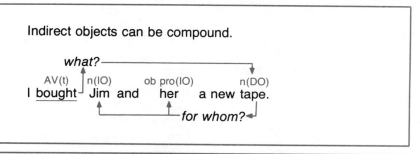

Words that precede a direct object or indirect object are the kinds that precede any noun or pronoun.

A

■ On a separate sheet write each of the sentences below.
■ Underline the verb or verb phrase.
■ Place parentheses around the prepositional phrases.
■ Label all words in the sentence.
■ Designate action verbs as transitive or intransitive. (Watch for linking verbs.)

1. The praise of her teachers gave Michele much pleasure.

2. You should ask your brother for help.

3. They had slept soundly in the back seat.

4. The police asked one of them many questions.

5. His wife's famous ancestor had also been exceptionally wealthy.

6. We sent those a copy of the contract.

7. He had also sent the extremely shy young lady a dozen roses.

8. The city council had promised the extremely irate citizens a substantial reduction in taxes.

B

■ On a separate sheet write each of the sentences below.
■ Underline the verb or verb phrase.
■ Place parentheses around the prepositional phrases.
■ Label all words in the sentence.
■ Designate action verbs as transitive or intransitive. (Watch for linking verbs.)

1. A few had made themselves dresses.

2. The chef threw several into the boiling water.

3. The last event will be the swimming contest.

4. The next convention will be in Kansas City.

5. Mr. Proudfoot assigned himself a very difficult project.

6. They bloomed beautifully in the window box this spring.

7. Mozart became famous at an early age.

8. These require a deposit of two dollars.

9. Her explanation gave me a better understanding of the situation.

The abbreviation *OC* is used to indicate *object complements*.

A third action verb complement is called the *object complement.* It follows and renames the direct object and answers the questions *what* or *whom* when asked after the direct object.

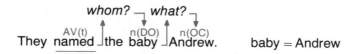

whom? — *what?*

They named the baby Andrew.   baby = Andrew

AV(t)   n(DO)   n(OC)

Object complements can also be adjectives. Such adjectives modify the direct object.

what? — *what?*

Nora thought the idea silly.   idea silly

AV(t)   n(DO)   adj(OC)

Indirect objects and direct objects do not rename each other as do direct objects and object complements.

what?

She bought him a wallet.   him ✕ wallet

AV(t)   ob pro(IO)   n(DO)

to whom?

A

■ Number your paper from 1 to 12.

■ Write the words that are nouns beside the corresponding number with the noun signal *the* in front of them. Label appropriately.

■ Write the words that are adjectives beside the corresponding number with the noun *people* or *things* after them. Label appropriately.

1. peculiarity
2. supporters
3. sick
4. genuine
5. outcome
6. enthused
7. unpainted
8. courses
9. qualified
10. demonstration
11. smart
12. beauty

■ On a separate sheet write the following pairs of sentences.
■ Underline the verb or verb phrase, and circle the two complements in each.
■ Determine if the two complements in each sentence are **DO** and **n(OC)** or **DO** and **adj(OC)**; label appropriately.

1. We found the sargeant pleasant.
2. We found him a dictator.

1. The students thought the program fun.
2. The teacher thought it a success.

1. The child believed the story true.
2. Everyone believed the tale a lie.

1. They found her a real winner.
2. They found her very reliable.

■ On a separate sheet write the following sentences.
■ Underline the verb or verb phrase, and circle the two complements in each.
■ Determine if the two complements in each sentence are **IO** and **DO** or **DO** and **OC**; label appropriately.

1. Everyone called me Curly.
2. He gave the custodian a nice raise.
3. Mother bought my sister some new glasses.
4. They elected her their new mayor.
5. All thought him a very intelligent person.
6. We bought ourselves new jogging shoes.
7. The company considers these their best salespeople.

- On a separate sheet write the following sentences.
- Underline the verb or verb phrase; designate action verbs as transitive or intransitive.
- Place parentheses around the prepositional phrases.
- Label all words in the sentence. (Watch for linking verbs.)

1. This says nothing.
2. The teachers thought them polite and intelligent.
3. My feet were really hurting after the parade.
4. My neighbor will pay Jeff two dollars for the job.
5. Her mother's oldest friend has remained a recluse.
6. The committee thought the last projects very worthwhile.
7. The boy renamed the horse Geronimo.
8. The turkey is smelling delicious.
9. She proved herself both competent and dependable.

- On a separate sheet write the following sentences.
- Underline the verb or verb phrase; designate action verbs as transitive or intransitive.
- Place parentheses around the prepositional phrases.
- Label all words in the sentence. (Watch for linking verbs.)

1. The university made her an associate professor.
2. His speech will be the big event of the evening.
3. They are moving to Puerto Rico this week.
4. The audience gave the performer a standing ovation.
5. Everyone finds the food and service excellent.
6. The new rules allow each player three minutes.
7. Susanne's twin is shorter.
8. Miss Chung praised the stage crew and the cast.
9. We believe these completely reliable.
10. The mayor then appointed Mr. Alvarez director of our division.

An *imperative sentence* expresses a direct command or request. The subject of such a sentence is always the pronoun *you,* but it is usually not expressed.

(S)   AV
You   Hurry to the store.

(S)   AV
You   Meet me at the cafeteria.

Imperative sentences with action verbs have the usual complements.

(S)   AV(t) n(DO)
You   Tell   Ruth (about the party).

(S)   AV(t) ob pro(IO)   n(DO)
You   Hand   him   the hammer.

(S)   aux adv AV(t) n(DO) adj(OC)
You   Do n't think Hank   rude.

Linking verb sentences can also be imperative.

(S)   LV   n(PN)
You   Be a good sport.

(S)   LV   P Adj
You   Look alert.

(S)   LV   P Adv
You   Be (on time).

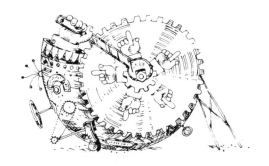

A

- On a separate sheet write the sentences below.
- Underline the verb or verb phrase.
- Place parentheses around the prepositional phrases.
- Label all words appropriately.

1. Take this letter to your mother.
2. Don't paint that wall blue.
3. Be there.
4. Give us your answer by tomorrow.
5. Elect them your new representatives.
6. Remain quiet.
7. Keep her calm and happy.
8. Run for the house.
9. Be the best!
10. Stop!

B

- On a separate sheet write the sentences below.
- Underline the verb or verb phrase.
- Place parentheses around the prepositional phrases.
- Label all words appropriately.

1. Give them a rest.
2. Get into the back seat.
3. Be careful.
4. Keep yourself physically fit.
5. Pay them the minimum wage.
6. Loan her your math book.
7. Be my guest.
8. Appoint someone the chairperson.
9. Be early.
10. Report to Mr. Goldberg's department.

The Simple Sentence

REVIEW A

■ Using the blanks and abbreviations below as a guide, write appropriate original sentences on a sheet of paper.

		S	AV	n(DO)			S	AV	d pro(DO)
1.	**a.**	___	___	___ .	**d.**	___	___	___	___ .
		S	AV	ob pro(DO)			S	AV	r pro(DO)
	b.	___	___	___ .	**e.**	___	___	___ .
		S	AV	id pro(DO)
	c.	___	___	___ .

		S	AV	n(IO)	cj	ob pro(IO)	n(DO)
2.	**a.**	___	___	___	___	___ a	___ .
		S	AV	ob pro(IO)	cj	id pro(IO)	n(DO)
	b.	___	___	___	___	___ the	___ .
		S	AV	r pro(IO)	n(DO)
	c.	___	___	___ a	___ .

		S	AV	n(DO)	n(OC)
3.	**a.**	___	___	___ a	___ .
		S	AV	ob pro(DO)	adj(OC)
	b.	___	___	___ very	___ .

REVIEW B

■ On a sheet of paper, write the words that complete the following sentences.

1. The three kinds of linking verb complements are _____ _____ , _____ _____ , and _____ _____ .

2. The three kinds of action verb complements are _____ _____ , _____ _____ , and _____ _____ .

3. Adverbs answer the following questions: _____ , _____ , and _____ .

4. Adverbs can modify _____ , _____ , and other _____ .

5. A predicate nominative renames the _____ .

6. A predicate adjective modifies the _____ .

7. A predicate adverb can be one word, _____ _____ , or a _____ _____ .

8. A direct object can be found by asking _____ or _____ after an _____ _____ .

9. An indirect object can be found by asking _____ _____ or _____ , or _____ _____ or _____ .

10. An object complement renames or modifies a _____ _____ .

REVIEW C

■ On a sheet of paper, copy each of the following sentences, correcting any incorrect pronouns as you do so.
■ Label all words.

1. She and me will be there.
2. The last ones were him and I.
3. The clerk assisted Akira and I.
4. The pie was made for you and she.
5. The first contestants will be her and me.
6. I sent the copies to Julia and he.
7. The boss and they are away.
8. The secretary called he and us.

■ Copy the following sentences on the same sheet of paper.
■ Label all words.

1. The man was a schoolteacher.
2. He was very intelligent.
3. He is in his classroom during the morning.
4. He gave many tests.
5. He lectured about the nation's current problems.
6. He mailed me my grades.
7. He considered my sister a very good student.
8. He thought your situation critical.
9. Where is the math book?
10. Bring it with you.

REVIEW D

■ Copy the following sentences on a sheet of paper.
■ Label all words in the sentences.

1. Is she your sister?
2. Are the invitations ready?
3. Have Jill's parents been to New York?
4. Will the banker lend him the money?
5. When can the students leave?
6. Did you think the car a good buy?
7. Have these studied their science?
8. Which one's car is still running well?

1. The boss was in a bad mood.
2. The bear smelled the skunk.
3. The skunk smelled horrible.
4. My mother has always been very beautiful.
5. Jimmy has become an excellent swimmer.
6. Stir slowly.
7. When was the deadline?
8. She proved herself extremely capable.
9. After lunch we rested.
10. The president named him his aide.

REVIEW E

■ Number your paper from 1 to 8.
■ Beside the corresponding number, identify the underlined word as predicate nominative, predicate adjective, predicate adverb, direct object, indirect object, or object complement.

A. 1. The maid had moved the <u>furniture</u>.
2. Mr. Chin sent <u>me</u> a copy.
3. They are the best rock <u>group</u> today.

4. Both of them were gold medal <u>winners</u>.

5. My little brother is <u>nice</u> at times.

6. <u>Here</u> are the salad forks.

7. I gave my <u>aunt</u> a basket of fruit.

8. This job would be <u>easy</u> for you.

B. 1. A sunny day would be a welcome <u>change</u>.

2. The police asked the suspect many <u>questions</u>.

3. Rebecca is practicing her <u>part</u> in the play.

4. The time is <u>now</u>!

5. Do the students have their <u>books</u>?

6. Mrs. Butler is making <u>herself</u> a sweater.

7. Both are well-trained <u>gymnasts</u>.

8. Neither of them will be <u>eligible</u>.

C. 1. This chemical turned the water <u>purple</u>.

2. Terry is not very <u>tall</u>.

3. Norbert's idea sounds <u>good</u> to me.

4. The store won't exchange <u>these</u>.

5. Could one of these be the right <u>key</u>?

6. <u>Where</u> are the lemons?

7. The letter promised her an <u>interview</u>.

8. They have become best <u>friends</u>.

D. 1. Is your sister a <u>sophomore</u>?

2. The mail is <u>here</u>.

3. He offered the customer a big <u>reduction</u>.

4. The water here tastes <u>strange</u> to me.

5. Success made Sylvia <u>snobbish</u>.

6. His daughter is becoming a <u>lawyer</u>.

7. Hide <u>them</u>!

8. The error remained <u>unnoticed</u>.

E. 1. Angela opened her <u>folder</u>.

2. Before the game all the players looked <u>tense</u>.

3. The truth is his <u>goal</u>.

4. <u>There</u> are the tests.

5. Do you have an extra <u>pencil</u>?

6. All have been active <u>members</u> in our committee.

7. The teacher called the story a <u>romance</u>.

8. My stepfather is very <u>talented</u>.

REVIEW F

■ On a sheet of paper, determine the use of the underlined pronouns in the sentences below by writing the appropriate letter next to the corresponding number.

   a. Object of preposition (Object Pronoun)
   b. Direct object, indirect object (Object Pronoun)
   c. Subject (Nominative Pronoun)
   d. Predicate nominative (Nominative Pronoun)

■ If the correct pronoun form is used, write **C**; write **I** if incorrect.

A. 1. He loaned the car to Ann and <u>she</u>.

2. Susanne and <u>me</u> are seniors.

3. The last ones to class were Fred and <u>he</u>.

4. I gave Jeff and <u>she</u> a copy of the script.

5. We and <u>they</u> will be opponents.

B. 1. She and <u>us</u> will be there.

2. The best swimmers were you and <u>me</u>.

3. The clerk was assisting Kim and <u>him</u>.

4. The pie was made for you and <u>her</u>.

5. The secretary called him and <u>I</u>.

C. 1. I sent Julia and <u>him</u> an invitation.

2. The boss and <u>them</u> are away.

3. I and the others will be ready.

4. The best performers are Sybil and she.

5. They waited for you and he for twenty minutes.

D. 1. My father and me are leaving today.

2. The teacher gave Tim and I extra points.

3. She wrote a letter to Sue and she.

4. The best acrobats were Rob and we.

5. The coach instructed Tony and he in boxing.

E. 1. Were Todd and she here?

2. They danced with Kim and me.

3. The best teams have always been them and us.

4. Give Mike and him the keys.

5. Mary, Dawn, and me are the new cheerleaders.

F. 1. The janitor complained about Rick and I.

2. The new members are they and Tom.

3. Both you and them can represent the group

4. The contract promised he and us a good raise.

5. The team disappointed themselves and him.

REVIEW G

- ■ Copy the following sentences on a sheet of paper.
- ■ Underline the verbs and verb phrases.
- ■ Put parentheses around all prepositional phrases.
- ■ Label all words in the sentences, indicating whether action verbs are transitive or intransitive.

1. Later write them a note of thanks.

2. The lemon sauce for the carrot pudding should not taste either too tart or too sweet.

3. Both the gowns and diplomas for our seniors' graduation will be delivered there.

4. In the afternoons and evenings the Siggins' daughters have worked at their jobs, studied for school, practiced their music, and helped out at home.

5. This winter my usual escape from the pressures of my business will be skiing at Vail.

6. Did they elect them our new representatives?

7. Some are sounding neither enthusiastic nor optimistic.

8. Now these are on my mind.

9. I still believe the truck driver innocent.

10. Who can be finished by lunchtime?

11. The somewhat eccentric but very rich old man left his only grandson the entire fortune.

REVIEW H

■ Copy the following sentences on a sheet of paper.
■ Underline the verbs and verb phrases.
■ Place parentheses around all prepositional phrases.
■ Label all words in the sentences, indicating whether the action verbs are transitive or intransitive.

1. Since September which students have dropped out of band?

2. This is the last one of either's collection.

3. These experiences have made his personality somewhat warped.

4. Be smart and save some of your money.

5. He hadn't considered his totally unreliable son good material for the extremely demanding job.

6. Someone's calculations must somehow have been faulty.

7. Either one of the witnesses or someone in his company sent the judge and both lawyers a devastating piece of evidence.

8. It doesn't usually smell so terrible.

9. Where are the punch bowl and ladle?

10. Can she become that with her rather limited natural abilities and her dislike for hard work?

GRAMMAR

STEP-BY-STEP

UNIT/I

The Compound Sentence

UNIT II

The Compound Sentence

SKILL 1

Identifying Compound Sentences Containing Main Clauses Joined by Conjunctions

A group of words containing a subject and a verb is called a *clause*. See the examples below.

               n(S)   LV P Adv
although the race was over   (clause)

             n(S)   AV   n(DO)
when the clock struck three   (clause)

The above groups of words are clauses; however, they are <u>not</u> sentences. They do not express a complete thought.

A clause expressing a complete thought is called a *main clause.* See the example below.

Main Clause

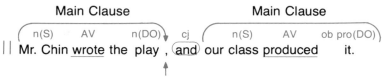

```
        n(S)    aux      LV                    PA
| The subject  is  becoming  more interesting.
```

A sentence like the one above that contains <u>one main clause</u> is called a *simple sentence.*

A sentence containing <u>two main clauses</u> joined by a <u>conjunction</u> is called a *compound sentence.* See below.

```
          Main Clause                        Main Clause
      n(S)     AV        n(DO)   cj      n(S)      AV      ob pro(DO)
|| Mr. Chin wrote  the  play ,  and  our class  produced      it.
```

A comma (,) usually follows the first clause of a compound sentence and immediately precedes the conjunction.

When the clauses of a compound sentence are very short, the comma after the first clause can be omitted.

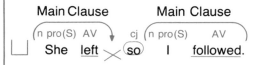

```
  Main Clause          Main Clause
 n pro(S) AV        cj  n pro(S)    AV
  She   left    so   I    followed.
```

A series (three or more) of very short main clauses can be separated by commas. Note below.

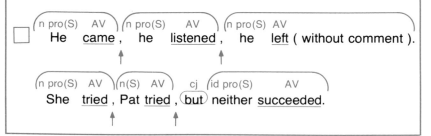

```
 n pro(S)   AV     n pro(S)    AV    n pro(S) AV
  He   came ,  he  listened ,  he   left ( without comment ).

 n pro(S)   AV    n(S)  AV   cj  id pro(S)       AV
 She  tried , Pat tried ,  but  neither  succeeded.
```

IMPORTANT

A compound subject or compound verb should not be mistaken for a compound sentence. Study the sentences below.

     n(S)   cj n(S) LV   n(PN)
Chris and Lee were a nuisance (at the class party).

Compound Subject

    n pro(S)   AV   cj   AV
They whistled or shouted (for hours).

Compound Verb

Conjunctions that most frequently connect clauses of a compound sentence are the following:

and	for	so
but	or	yet

CHECKUP

On a sheet of paper, write the answers to the questions below.

1. What is a clause?
2. What is a main clause?
3. What is a simple sentence?
4. What is a compound sentence?
5. Where is the comma placed in a typical compound sentence?
6. When is a comma unnecessary in a compound sentence?
7. How is a sentence containing a series of short main clauses punctuated?

A

■ On a separate sheet of paper, follow the instructions below.
■ Use the symbols before each set of instructions to find help on the preceding pages.

| 1. Write a simple sentence (one main clause) with a single subject and a single verb. Label all principal parts of the sentence (subject, verb, and complement).

2. Write a simple sentence with a compound subject. Label all principal parts of the sentence.

3. Write a simple sentence with a compound verb or verb phrase. Label all principal parts.

4. Write a compound sentence with two main clauses joined by the conjunction *and, but,* or *or.* Punctuate correctly, and label all principal parts.

5. Write a compound sentence with two main clauses joined by the conjunction *for, so,* or *yet.* Punctuate correctly and label all principal parts.

6. Write a compound sentence that does not require a comma. Label all principal parts.

7. Write a compound sentence containing a series of short main clauses. Punctuate correctly, and label all principal parts.

B

- On a separate sheet beside the corresponding number, write and label the principal parts in each sentence below and any conjunction connecting main clauses.
- Underline the verbs or verb phrases.
- Punctuate correctly.
- Indicate before each number whether the sentence is simple **(sp)** or compound **(cp).**

EXAMPLE: We had car trouble so I was late to school this morning.

          n pro(S) AV n(DO)   cj n pro(S) LV P Adj
cp **1.** We <u>had</u> trouble, so   I   <u>was</u> late.

1. A few came with serious doubts but left with an improved outlook.

2. No one was lost in the flood but property damage ran extremely high.

3. Herman prepared the refreshments and Heidi planned the activities.

4. The wind and rain battered and actually disabled the vessel.

5. Both you and I should try a different approach to our problem.

6. He could not pay for the meal for he had lost his wallet.

7. The manager roared the cook quit and the waiter cried.

8. The school will be adding a new auditorium and remodeling the gym.

9. She can call the doctor tomorrow or she can make an appointment.

10. The rather distinguished gentleman and his companion went into the station and vanished before our eyes.

11. He called and she answered the phone.

12. Lillian sang Jordan played his flute and we danced.

C

- On a separate sheet beside the corresponding number, write and label the principal parts in each sentence below and any conjunction connecting main clauses.
- Underline the verbs or verb phrases.
- Punctuate correctly.
- Indicate before each number whether the sentence is simple **(sp)** or compound **(cp)**.

1. Some left the meeting and didn't return until the afternoon session.

2. Her car was the oldest one in the race but it won easily.

3. Both freshmen and sophomores are taking reading tests today.

4. Continue to the next corner and go six blocks to your right.

5. Rebecca graduates this spring so she is busy with her college plans.

6. Tim was chosen for a part for he was extremely good at tryouts.

7. Several asked but he declined.

8. Many of them were impassable so we cancelled the rehearsal.

9. He danced she sang and the audience hissed.

10. Those were excellent players yet none compared to you.

11. They left so I retired early.

12. Dad and Elena washed and polished both cars Saturday.

SKILL TEST

■ On a separate sheet beside the corresponding number, write and label the principal parts in each sentence below and any conjunction connecting main clauses.
■ Underline the verbs or verb phrases.
■ Punctuate correctly.
■ Indicate before each number whether the sentence is simple **(sp)** or compound **(cp)**.

1. The lights dimmed the performer entered and the audience gasped.

2. Both body and mind must be fed properly.

3. These and several of those fell during the quake and were broken.

4. Both of his parents died in the crash so his mother's sister reared him.

5. They can't go but I can manage it.

6. Dolores wouldn't agree to the idea for she could anticipate its tragic consequences.

7. Sunshine is abundant here in Florida and tourists often visit during the winter.

8. Flying squirrels don't really fly but glide from tree to tree.

SKILL 2

Identifying Compound Sentences Containing Clauses Joined by Conjunctive Adverbs

The letters *cj adv* are used to indicate *conjunctive adverbs.*

In formal writing a longer connective is sometimes used to connect clauses in a compound sentence. Study the examples below.

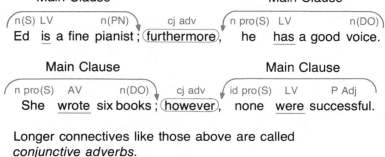

Main Clause   Main Clause

   n(S)   LV   n(PN)   cj adv   n pro(S)   LV   n(DO)
Ed   is a fine pianist ; furthermore,   he   has a good voice.

Main Clause   Main Clause

  n pro(S)   AV   n(DO)   cj adv   id pro(S)   LV   P Adj
  She   wrote six books ; however,   none   were successful.

Longer connectives like those above are called *conjunctive adverbs.*

Two marks of punctuation are necessary when clauses are joined by conjunctive adverbs. Study the example below.

Main Clause		Main Clause

n(S) LV   n(PN)   cj adv   n(S) aux aux   AV
Friday is Veterans' Day ; (consequently), banks will be closed.

Note that a semicolon (;) follows the first clause, and a comma (,) follows the conjunctive adverb.

The most frequently used conjunctive adverbs are:

also	moreover
consequently	nevertheless
furthermore	otherwise
however	therefore

CHECKUP

On a sheet of paper, write the answers to the questions below.

1. When are two different marks of punctuation needed in forming a compound sentence?
2. Where are these marks placed in the sentence?
3. Name eight conjunctive adverbs.

A list of these conjunctions appears on page 71.

■ Study the list of conjunctions that connect clauses of a compound sentence.
■ Without referring to the list, write them on a separate sheet. Use the letters below as clues.

a__, b__, f__, o__, s__, y__

■ Study the list of conjunctive adverbs that connect clauses of a compound sentence.
■ Without referring to the list, write them on a separate sheet.

a__, c__, f__, h__, m__, n__, o__, t__

C

■ On a separate sheet of paper, write sentences to fit the formulas below.
■ Punctuate where necessary.

1.
 n(S)　　LV　　ps pro　n(PN)　cj adv　n pro(S)　AV　　adj　　n(DO)
 ＿＿＿　＿＿＿　＿＿＿　＿＿＿　＿＿＿　＿＿＿　＿＿＿　＿＿＿　＿＿＿ .

2.
 id pro(S)　LV　　P Adj　cj adv　n(S)　　AV　　　p　　n(OP)
 ＿＿＿　＿＿＿　＿＿＿　＿＿＿　＿＿＿　＿＿＿　（ ＿＿＿　＿＿＿ ）.

3.
 n(S)　　AV　　n(IO)　　adj　　n(DO)　　cj　id pro(S)　adv　　LV　　P Adv
 ＿＿＿　＿＿＿　＿＿＿　＿＿＿　＿＿＿　＿＿＿　＿＿＿　＿＿＿　＿＿＿　＿＿＿ .

D

■ On a separate sheet beside the corresponding number, write and label the principal parts and any words that connect main clauses in each sentence below.
■ Underline the verbs or verb phrases.
■ Punctuate correctly.
■ Indicate before each number whether the sentence is simple **(sp)** or compound **(cp).**

1. The editor should have determined the cost and then notified me.

2. Most of the citizens enthusiastically voted her the town's new mayor also they named the new hospital after her.

3. The best sale will be next week but I will be on vacation.

4. It was someone in a yellow car furthermore the license plates were missing.

5. I go or she stays.

6. The Spanish examination was very difficult however the history test was an easy one.

7. The time for action has arrived consequently we must stop this debate immediately.

8. The ones for the head table are these and those belong on the stage.

9. The judge had patiently heard and had subsequently rejected everyone's plea.

■ On a separate sheet beside the corresponding number, write and label the principal parts and any words that connect main clauses in each sentence below.

■ Underline the verbs or verb phrases.

■ Punctuate correctly.

■ Indicate before each number whether the sentence is simple **(sp)** or compound **(cp).**

1. He worked hard for reelection however the other candidate beat him by a large majority.

2. Both Rene and I have dental appointments this morning otherwise we would accompany you to the library.

3. Everybody can either call me or put a note in my box.

4. The professor thought Mr. Carver's son very talented on the violin therefore she constantly gave him extra encouragement.

5. Our host was gracious the food was excellent and the conversation was stimulating.

6. The siren sounded and everyone stopped abruptly.

7. My somewhat abrasive letter was in the mail consequently I could only wait for the reaction.

8. Neither the mail delivery nor the school buses could move for the streets were flooded and blocked for miles.

SKILL TEST

■ On a separate sheet beside the corresponding number, write and label the principal parts and any words that connect main clauses in each sentence below.
■ Underline the verbs or verb phrases.
■ Punctuate correctly.
■ Indicate before each number whether the sentence is simple **(sp)** or compound **(cp)**.

1. Last year the owner promised several a bonus but none ever became actual recipients.

2. He is the man on the right side of the picture and I am on his left.

3. The school flag had been burned moreover litter was scattered everywhere.

4. We just voted Ms. Carmendale our club's next president also she has been elected our city's representative.

5. Many of the prizes were donated by local merchants however recently other groups have generously given us many items.

6. Either the first or second judging will be tomorrow morning consequently everyone's entry must be labeled tonight.

7. The class had applied but had not received its license.

8. I asked and he readily gave his permission.

SKILL 3

Using Semicolons to Separate Main Clauses in Compound Sentences

When the two main clauses of a compound sentence are closely related in meaning, a semicolon alone can be used to separate the two clauses. Study the sentences below.

Main Clause   Main Clause

| They failed both tests badly ; they had not prepared.

Main Clause   Main Clause

The car coughed and coasted to a stop ; it was out of gas.

When a main clause of a compound sentence contains commas, a semicolon replaces the usual comma before the conjunction. Compare the sentences below.

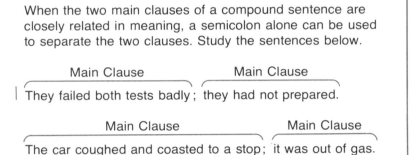

He brought me flowers , but I prefer diamonds.

Ted , Art , and Craig brought me flowers ; but I prefer diamonds.

I prefer diamonds ; but they brought me flowers , perfume , and candy.

CHECKUP

On a separate sheet of paper, write the answers to the questions below.

1. When can a semicolon alone be used to separate the clauses of a compound sentence?
2. When is a semicolon placed before the conjunction connecting two clauses of a compound sentence?

A

| **1.** Write a compound sentence with the main clauses closely related in meaning and separated by a semicolon alone. Use the symbol if necessary to find help on the previous page.

|| **2.** Write a compound sentence with the main clauses joined by a semicolon and a conjunction. Write a compound subject in the first clause consisting of three nouns. Use the symbol if necessary to find help on the previous page.

||| **3.** Write a compound sentence with the main clauses joined by a semicolon and a conjunction. Write three direct objects in the second main clause. Use the symbol if necessary to find help on the previous page.

B

■ On a separate sheet of paper complete the following sentences:

1. A semicolon alone can be used to separate the two clauses of a compound sentence when _____ .

2. A semicolon replaces the usual comma before the conjunction connecting clauses in a compound sentence when _____ .

C

■ On a separate sheet write the conjunctions that can connect clauses of compound sentences.

a___, b___, f___, o___, s___, y___

D

■ Write the conjunctive adverbs that can connect clauses of compound sentences.

a___, c___, f___, h___, m___, n___, o___, t___

CONCEPTS

Below are graphic formulas representing the concepts that you have studied in this unit. As a review of compound sentences, look at each formula sentence and try to recall the type of sentence each represents. If you have any difficulty, turn back to the appropriate section and review it before going further.

Simple Sentence

1. Main Clause.

Compound Sentences

1. Main Clause , cj Main Clause.

2. Main (, ,) Clause ; cj Main Clause.

3. Main Clause ; cj adv , Main Clause.

4. Main Clause ; Main Clause.

5. Main Clause ⨯ cj Main Clause.

6. Main Clause , Main Clause , cj Main Clause.

REVIEW A

■ On a separate sheet of paper, write sentences to fit the formulas presented in the preceding Concepts section.

Simple Sentence

1.

Compound Sentences

1.   4.

2.   5.

3.   6.

REVIEW B

■ On a separate sheet of paper, complete the following sentences.

1. A group of words is called a clause when _____.
2. A clause is called a main clause when _____.
3. A sentence is a simple sentence when _____.
4. A sentence is a compound sentence when _____.
5. A _____ is required before the conjunction connecting clauses of a compound sentence.
6. No mark of punctuation is necessary after the first clause of a compound sentence when _____.
7. _____ separate a series of very short main clauses.
8. A _____ is required before a conjunctive adverb and a _____ after it when joining clauses in a compound sentence.
9. A semicolon alone can be used to separate the two clauses of a compound sentence when _____.
10. A semicolon replaces the usual comma before the conjunction connecting clauses in a compound sentence when _____.

REVIEW C

■ On a separate sheet beside the corresponding number, write and label the principal parts and any words that connect main clauses in each sentence below.
■ Underline the verbs or verb phrases.
■ Punctuate correctly.
■ Indicate before each number whether the sentence is simple (sp) or compound (cp).

1. Several of them sent us their applications however we found them very young for this company's highly skilled operation.
2. We hesitated we debated we couldn't make the decision.
3. No one could agree on the theme for Homecoming nevertheless progress was made on other details concerning the event.

4. Both these paintings and those were carefully evaluated by our experts and chosen for the display.

5. They fought but they lost.

6. The committee selected her the winner of the scholarship for she was excellent in academics and athletics.

7. He remains an avid Cowboys' fan he would never miss one of their games.

8. Neither Andrea Lydia nor Martin were here so we saved them a few samples.

9. Have the painters scraped and painted the side of the building?

GRAMMAR

STEP-BY-STEP

UNIT XII

Words, Phrases, and Clauses Used as Nouns

UNIT III

Words, Phrases, and Clauses Used as Nouns

SKILL 1

Identifying Gerunds as Nouns

A *gerund* (pronounced jer′ und) is a verb ending in *ing* (eat<u>ing</u>, swimm<u>ing</u>, remain<u>ing</u>) used in a sentence as a noun. Study the sentences below.

n pro(S) aux   AV
He   is studying now.   <u>Studying</u> is a verb.

ger-n(S)   aux aux   AV
Studying will be required.   <u>Studying</u> is a gerund.

Gerunds are never preceded by auxiliary verbs. Action verbs in their *ing* forms are always preceded by auxiliary verbs.

The abbreviation used to indicate *gerunds* is *ger*.

Gerunds not only function as <u>subjects</u> but also as <u>predicate nominatives</u>. Remember that predicate nominatives can change places with the subject without changing the meaning of the sentence. Study the sentences below.

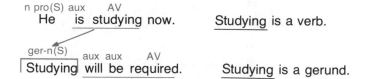

ger-n(S) LV   n(PN)
I Reading is her best subject.

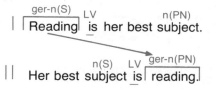

n(S) LV ger-n(PN)
II Her best subject is reading.

Gerunds can also function as <u>objects of prepositions</u>.

      n pro(S)   AV   n(DO)   p ger-n(OP)
      He   <u>devoted</u> his life (to| teaching.|)

      p   ger-n(OP)   n(S)   LV P Adj
    (For| relaxing|), these clothes <u>are</u> ideal.

Gerunds can also function as <u>objects of action verbs</u>.

what?

    n pro(S) AV   ger-n(DO)
    I   <u>love</u> | skiing.|

what?   *what?*

    n(S)   AV   ger-n(DO)   n(OC)
  The group <u>chose</u> | bicycling| their mode (of travel.)

what?   *what?*

    n(S)   AV   ger-n(DO) adj(OC)
  Father <u>thinks</u>| traveling| tiresome.

what?

    n(S)   AV   ger-n(IO)   n(DO)
  Mother <u>gives</u>| gardening her best efforts.
             — *to what?*

Gerunds may be preceded by the same modifiers that come before any noun (noun signals, adjectives, adverbs, noun adjuncts). Study the sentences below.

    s ps n ger-n(S) aux   AV
    Nora's| bowling| <u>is improving</u>.

    n pro(S)   AV   ps pro ger-n(DO) adv adj(OC)
    We   <u>deemed</u> his | cooking| very delicious.

    n(S)   AV   p ps id pro ger-n(OP)
  Success <u>depends</u> (on everyone's| working.|)

    adj n(S)   AV   adv adj n adj ger-n(DO)
  The coach <u>demanded</u> very good ball| playing.|

IMPORTANT

Do not forget that an *ing* word can be the verb of the sentence when the subject performs the action. Note below.

n(S) aux   AV

○ The band is practicing.

CHECKUP

Answer the questions below on a sheet of paper.

1. What are gerunds?
2. How can they function in sentences?
3. What kinds of words can precede gerunds?
4. What kind of words can never precede a gerund?
5. When is an *ing* word a predicate nominative?
6. When is an *ing* word the verb of the sentence?

A

■ On a separate sheet complete the sentences by furnishing an appropriate gerund.
■ If necessary, use the symbols to find help on the previous pages.

| 1.
ger-n(S) LV   n(PN)
_____ was his profession.

|| 2.
           n(S) LV ger-n(PN)
Her best sport is _____

3.
(S)
n pro   AV   n(DO)   p ger-n(OP)
He bought new shoes (for _____.)

4.
      n(S)   AV(t)   ger-n(DO)
The law prohibited _____ .

5.
(S)
n pro   AV   ger-n(DO)   adj(OC)
I consider _____ very unrefined.

6.
    n(S) AV(t) ger-n(DO)   n(OC)
The law makes _____ a crime.

7.
     n(S) AV(t) ger-n(IO)   n(DO)
The artist gave _____ her complete consideration.

8.
ps n
Rebecca's

ps pro
His

ps id pro
Neither's

ger-n(S) AV(t)   n(DO)
_____ won a gold medal.

B

- On a separate sheet of paper, follow the directions below.
- Use the symbols to refer back to appropriate examples if necessary.

| 1. Write a sentence using a gerund as the subject.

|| 2. Write a sentence using a gerund as a predicate nominative.

3. Write a sentence using a gerund as an object of a preposition.

4. Write a sentence using a gerund as the direct object.

5. Write a sentence using a gerund as a direct object followed by an object complement that is a noun.

6. Write a sentence using a gerund as a direct object followed by an object complement that is an adjective.

7. Write a sentence using a gerund as an indirect object.

8. Write a sentence with a gerund preceded by a noun adjunct.

9. Write a sentence with a gerund preceded by an adjective and an adverb.

10. Write a sentence with an *ing* word used as the action verb of the sentence.

C

- In each pair of sentences below, the *ing* word is a predicate nominative in one, an action verb in the other.
- Number your paper from 1 to 10.
- Beside the corresponding number, write the function (**AV** or **PN**) of each underlined word.
  (Remember that a predicate nominative can be exchanged with the subject without changing the meaning of the sentence.)

1. The best exercise is <u>jogging</u>.

2. The best athlete is <u>jogging</u>.

3. His favorite friend was <u>fishing</u>.

4. His favorite sport was <u>fishing</u>.

5. Mom's worst chore is <u>ironing</u>.

6. Mom's neighbor was <u>ironing</u>.

7. His childhood problem had been <u>lying</u>.

8. The oldest child had been <u>lying</u>.

9. My latest interest is <u>advertising</u>.

10. Many in my business are <u>advertising</u>.

11. I was <u>shopping</u> for a new umbrella.

12. My aunt's main diversion is <u>shopping</u>.

D

- On a separate sheet write the sentences below.
- Underline the verb or verb phrase.
- Place parentheses around the prepositional phrases.
- Draw a bracket above the gerunds and label appropriately.
- Label all words.
- If necessary, use the symbols to find help on the preceding pages.

1. The next step is refinishing.

2. Smoking was forbidden by law.

3. Andrea enjoys horseback riding.

4. Everyone gave studying too little time.

5. They thought working repulsive.

6. The monkeys have been chattering for hours.

7. Those were bad in the beginning.

1. Her roommate always does her studying.

2. He will receive a trophy for winning.

3. My father taught me diving.

4. These are falling.

5. Sleeping will be difficult.

6. Their best talent was singing.

7. Some consider rope jumping the best exercise.

■ On a separate sheet of paper, number from 1 to 8.
■ Beside the corresponding number, write each word in the sentence ending in *ing*.
■ After each word write its function in the sentence (**S, PN, DO, AV,** etc.)

1. Dancing is my favorite recreation.

2. His worst fault was complaining.

3. The band soon began its playing.

4. The wrestling was during the afternoon.

5. Both Michelle and I gave swimming our best efforts.

6. These are my best shoes for long distance running.

7. One explained the techniques of rug weaving.

8. She is making sandwiches for our picnic.

1. Take two aspirin before retiring.

2. My brother's cigarette smoking is harmful to his singing.

3. Our family has made hiking our hobby.

4. Their first objective will be winning.

5. Someone's steaks are burning.

6. Fast driving makes grandmother nervous.

7. You must give practicing more time.

8. Not only Wayne but also Nathan did some very good playing.

■ On a separate sheet write the sentences below.
■ Underline the verb or verb phrase.
■ Place parentheses around the prepositional phrases.
■ Label all principal parts; draw brackets above gerunds and label appropriately.
■ Punctuate where necessary.

1. My married brother is building near us and my parents think this situation great.

2. The voting ended and everyone left.

3. The award was given for wrestling however he is equally good in boxing.

4. Unfortunately she makes eating her first love.

5. I appreciate most their expert tailoring nevertheless all of their work is very satisfactory.

6. The swimming was good the games were fun and Mrs. Yen's cooking was most enjoyable.

7. The teacher scolded them sternly but they couldn't stop laughing.

8. Give his sculpturing a close examination.

9. Helping makes her happy so I assign her many little tasks.

10. The rule prohibits gum chewing nevertheless he constantly ignores it.

11. Evaluating was difficult.

SKILL TEST

- On a separate sheet write the sentences below.
- Underline the verb or verb phrase.
- Place parentheses around the prepositional phrases.
- Label all principal parts; draw brackets above gerunds and label appropriately.
- Punctuate where necessary.

1. Passing is your first objective but another worthwhile goal is learning.

2. She encouraged my joining however it wasn't right for me.

3. Before planting one should prepare the soil by fertilizing and cultivating.

4. Give the developing a little less time and the photographs will be much better.

5. The class's science demonstration will be continuing for several hours so we can return later.

6. We found the singing delightful also everyone's extremely good acting made the play a memorable one.

REVIEW

■ On a separate sheet write the sentences below choosing the correct pronoun(s).

■ Label all words in the sentence.

1. **a.** Phillip and **him** / **he** are coming here.

    b. Jill, **we** / **us,** and **them** / **they** will stay.

2. **a.** The candidates are **her** / **she** and **I** / **me.**

    b. The last ones were **we** / **us** and **they** / **them.**

3. **a.** The ball hit **him** / **he** or **she** / **her.**

    b. The officer wanted **they** / **them** and **we** / **us.**

4. **a.** The minstrels sang to **them** / **they** and **I** / **me.**

    b. For either **she** / **her** or **him** / **he** the job will be easy.

■ On a separate sheet write the sentences below replacing any incorrect pronoun with the correct form.

■ Label all words in the sentence.

1. The speech offended her and I.

2. The class officers were him and her.

3. The winners will play he and me.

4. They and us must plan better.

5. The donations were given by him and I.

SKILL 2

Identifying Gerund Phrases

Use the abbreviation *ger phr* to indicate a *gerund phrase.*

Because gerunds are verbs converted into nouns, they retain certain verb traits. They can be followed by complements (words that answer *who(m)* and *what*). Study the examples below.

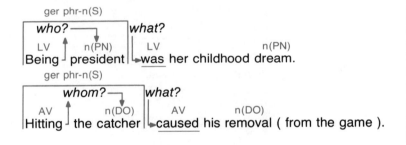

Gerunds, like verbs, can also be followed by <u>adverbs</u> (words that answer *how, when, where,* and *why*). Study the examples.

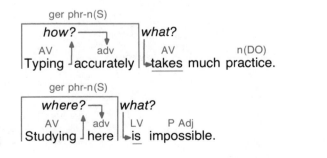

A single gerund can be followed by <u>complements, adverbs, and prepositional phrases</u>. Prepositional phrases usually respond to the adverb questions *how, when, where,* and *why.* Study the example below.

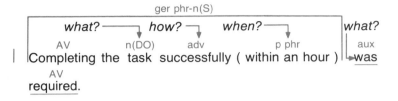

A gerund and the complements, adverbs, and prepositional phrases that accompany it constitute a *gerund phrase.* In the previous examples the entire gerund phrase is the subject of each sentence. Note that the bracket is drawn above the entire phrase.

Gerund phrases function not only as subjects but also as predicate nominatives. See below.

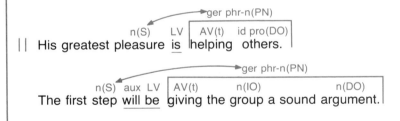

Gerund phrases also function as objects of verbs.

```
                                    ger phr-n(DO)
    n pro(S)      AV      ps pro | AV(t)      n(DO)
        I     appreciate   your  fixing my typewriter.
```

```
                              ger phr-n(DO)
    n(S)       AV      | AV(t)     n(DO)              n(OC)
    Mom   considered    doing housework  a rewarding occupation.
```

Gerund phrases also function as objects of prepositions.

```
                                              ger phr-n(OP)
 n pro(S) aux    AV      p  ┌──────────────────────────────────┐
                           │ AV(i)                              │
   I    am delighted ( about│ going ( with you ) ( to the dinner. )│
                           └──────────────────────────────────┘
                                             ger phr-n(OP)
 n pro(S)  AV    p  ┌──────────────────────────────────────────┐
                   │ AV(i)    adv    adj    n(DO)                │
   He    won ( by│ striking out  every batter ( for three innings. )│
                   └──────────────────────────────────────────┘
```

IMPORTANT

Remember that a gerund is *always* the first word in a gerund phrase.

IMPORTANT

Do not forget that an *ing* word is the verb of the sentence when the subject performs the action.

```
 n(S) aux  aux   AV      n(DO)
 Pat has been fixing my dress.
```

```
 n pro(S) aux  LV       P Adj
  You  are being very generous.
```

CHECKUP

Answer the questions below on a sheet of paper.

1. What is a gerund?
2. How can they function in sentences?
3. What kinds of words can precede them?
4. What constitutes a gerund phrase?
5. What six questions should be asked to find all complements and modifiers that are part of the gerund phrase?
6. What does a gerund phrase always begin with?

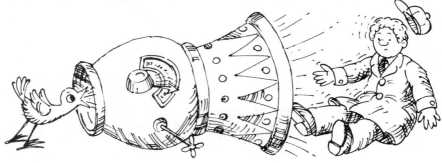

A

■ On a separate sheet complete the sentences below by furnishing the appropriate words.
■ Use the symbols if necessary to find help on pages 96–97.

1. **a.** Rob's ⎿ger-n(S)⏌ is LV (against the rules.) P Adv

   b. Rob's ⎿ger phr-n(S)⏌ is LV (against the rules.) P Adv

2. **a.** Her first task n(S) was LV ⎿ger-n(PN)⏌.

   b. Her first task n(S) was LV ⎿ger phr-n(PN)⏌.

3. **a.** I n pro(S) love AV ⎿ger-n(DO)⏌.

   b. I n pro(S) love AV ⎿ger phr-n(PN)⏌.

4. **a.** The group made n(S) AV ⎿ger-n(DO)⏌ a requirement n(OC) (for membership.)

   b. The group made n(S) AV ⎿ger phr-n(DO)⏌ a requirement n(OC) (for membership.)

5. **a.** The coach congratulated n(S) AV her ob pro(DO) (for p ⎿ger-n(OP)⏌.)

   b. The coach congratulated n(S) AV her ob pro(DO) (for p ⎿ger phr-n(OP)⏌.)

B

■ On a separate sheet of paper, follow the directions below.
■ Use the symbols to refer back to the examples on pages 96–97 if necessary.

1. Write a sentence using a gerund phrase as the subject.

2. Write a sentence using a gerund phrase as a predicate nominative.

3. Write a sentence using a gerund phrase as a direct object.

4. Write a sentence using a gerund phrase as a direct object followed by an object complement.

5. Write a sentence using a gerund phrase as an object of a preposition.

6. Write a sentence using the *ing* form of a verb as the verb of the sentence.

C

■ On a separate sheet write the sentences below.
■ Underline the verb or verb phrase.
■ Place parentheses around prepositional phrases.
■ Place a bracket above each gerund phrase, including in each phrase any complements, adverbs, or prepositional phrases.
■ Label the use of each phrase in the sentence; then label all other words in the sentence.
■ If necessary, use the symbols to find help on pages 96–97.

1. Parking here is illegal.
2. She tried fixing a fancy meal.
3. They are reconsidering their first decision.
4. His job is printing the local paper.
5. She was wise in awarding the sketch first prize.
6. My little chimp likes riding the bicycle.
7. He can be expecting them soon.
8. Everyone found shopping this year a nightmare.

1. Tonight we will be dining at Monty's.
2. Some delight in being facetious.
3. Playing football with my older brother is really fun.
4. They disliked paying for bad food.
5. I am running for mayor.
6. My niece has begun campaigning for me.
7. The usual topic of conversation is complaining about taxes.
8. Others found the ordering of supplies extremely tedious.

■ On a separate sheet of paper, write the sentences below.
■ Underline the verb or verb phrase.
■ Place parentheses around prepositional phrases.
■ Place a bracket above each gerund phrase, and label its use in the sentence.
■ Label the principal parts in each main clause.
■ Punctuate appropriately.

1. Working on Mondays will not be necessary therefore we will always have long weekends.

2. My brother was grounded for missing the bus so he is in his bedroom.

3. The rules prohibit students' keeping the equipment overnight nevertheless these circumstances certainly warrant an exception.

4. Elvira's worst problem is eating too much.

5. Reading expands the mind writing makes it exact.

6. We thought her winning the national title the greatest moment of her career but it was insignificant in comparison to her later accomplishments.

7. Our uncle has always been a very active person however since his illness he has been resting during the day.

■ On a separate sheet of paper, write the sentences below.
■ Underline the verb or verb phrase.
■ Place parentheses around prepositional phrases.
■ Place a bracket above each gerund phrase, and label its use in the sentence.
■ Label the principal parts in each main clause.
■ Punctuate appropriately.

1. The doctors consider his tennis playing a definite benefit to his health consequently he is playing regularly now.

2. Erika's walking with that bad ankle will be painful and harmful.

3. The speaking ended but the crowd remained.

4. Our fat cousins hated eating vegetables moreover they avoided doing any physical exercise.

5. One of my fears is forgetting my wife's birthday therefore I send her flowers every week.

6. My stepmother is giving the refinishing her detailed attention.

7. Losing their quarterback made their winning impossible.

SKILL TEST

- On a separate sheet of paper, write the sentences below.
- Underline the verb or verb phrase.
- Place parentheses around prepositional phrases.
- Place a bracket above each gerund phrase, and label its use in the sentence.
- Label the principal parts in each main clause.
- Punctuate appropriately.

1. My father didn't mind delivering my papers however his getting bitten by a dog wasn't his idea of a reward.

2. Everyone's daily routine was walking the dog in the park.

3. Football is over basketball hasn't begun but playing my records is keeping me content.

4. Some started singing the national anthem and all stood up.

5. The bank's president was giving them five dollars for washing her car every week so it always looked beautiful.

6. We should be doing our Christmas shopping.

SKILL 3

Identifying Infinitives and Infinitive Phrases Used as Nouns

Use the abbreviation *inf* to label *infinitives*.

An *infinitive* is a verb in its simplest form (without added endings) preceded by the preposition *to.* The following are examples of infinitives.

| to go | to remain | to think |
| to be | to build | to race |

An infinitive, like a gerund, can function as a noun.

inf-n(S)

| | AV | aux | LV | n(PN) |
| To argue | would be | a mistake. |

The letters *inf phr* are used to indicate an *infinitive phrase.*

An infinitive followed by modifiers and/or complements constitutes an *infinitive phrase.* Study the examples below.

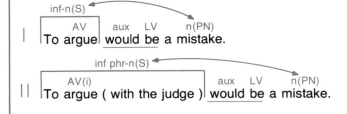

Infinitives and infinitive phrases function not only as subjects but also as predicate nominatives.

inf-n(PN)

n(S) LV AV
His desire is | to help.

inf phr-n(PN)

n(S) LV AV(t) ob pro(DO)
His desire is | to help   you   (with this problem.)

They also function as direct objects.

what?

n pro(S) AV inf-n(DO)
She tried─| AV
            to finish.

what?

n pro(S) AV inf phr-n(DO)
She tried─| AV(t)   n(DO)
            to finish the work (before noon.)

Sometimes an infinitive is preceded by a noun or pronoun that is part of the infinitive phrase. Such incidents occur only after action verbs when the infinitives serve as direct objects.

what?

inf phr-n(DO)
n(S)   AV   ob pro   LV P Adv
Dad expects─| (her) to be early.

what?

inf phr-n(DO)
n(S)   AV   id pro   LV P Adj
The chairperson asked─| (everyone) to be quiet.

what?

inf phr-n(DO)
n(S)   AV   n   LV   P Adv
Ms. Lopez required─| (students) to be (on time.)

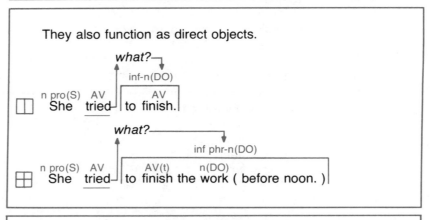

IMPORTANT

Any verb that functions as another part of speech is called a *verbal.* Gerunds and infinitives are verbals.

CHECKUP

Answer the questions below on a sheet of paper.

1. What is an infinitive?
2. What is an infinitive phrase?
3. How can infinitives and infinitive phrases be used in a sentence?
4. Under what circumstances do nouns and pronouns precede infinitives as part of infinitive phrases?
5. What is a gerund? What is a gerund phrase?
6. How can gerunds and gerund phrases be used in a sentence?
7. What are verbals?
8. What six questions should be asked to find all complements and modifiers that are part of the infinitive phrase?
9. Under what circumstances do nouns and pronouns precede infinitives as part of infinitive phrases?

■ On a separate sheet complete the following sentences by providing the appropriate words.
■ Use the symbols to find help on pages 102–103 if necessary.

| **1.** ☐ would be exciting.

inf-(S)   aux   LV   P Adj

|| **2.** ☐ would be exciting.

inf phr-n(S)   aux   LV   P Adj

☐ 3. The only solution <u>was</u> [n(S) LV inf-n(PN)].

The only solution <u>was</u> [ ].
n(S) *LV* *inf-n(PN)*

☐ 4. The only solution <u>was</u> [ ].
n(S) *LV* *inf phr-n(PN)*

☐ 5. They <u>hope</u> [ ].
n pro(S) *AV* *inf-n(DO)*

☐ 6. They <u>hope</u> [ ].
n pro(S) *AV* *inf phr-n(DO)*

○ 7. The boss <u>demanded</u> [n inf].
n(S) *AV* *inf phr-n(DO)*

B

■ On a separate sheet follow the directions below.
■ Use the symbols to refer back to the examples on pages 102–103 if necessary.

‖ 1. Write a sentence using an infinitive phrase as a subject.

☐ 2. Write a sentence using an infinitive phrase as a predicate nominative.

☐ 3. Write a sentence using an infinitive phrase as a direct object.

○ 4. Write a sentence in which a noun or pronoun precedes the infinitive phrase as part of the phrase.

C

■ On a separate sheet write the sentences below.
■ Underline the verbs and verb phrases.
■ Place parentheses around prepositional phrases.
■ Place a bracket above each infinitive or infinitive phrase, and label its use in the sentence.
■ Label other principal parts.
■ Use the symbols to find help on pages 102–103 if necessary.

☐ 1. We decided to ask for an additional two weeks.

| 2. To study is essential to good grades.

☐ 3. My advice would be to discontinue your efforts.

○ 4. The news report asked everybody to lock their doors.

☐ 5. Her last wish was to see you.

6. To continue this course will bring disaster.

7. The remedy could be to quit.

8. The old man attempted to stand.

1. To retreat is unthinkable.

2. I wanted to go.

3. To agree with her now would only cause problems later.

4. Everyone expected him to lose.

5. Her promise has been to return.

6. The children hated to go to bed.

7. The committee's decision was to cancel the affair.

8. The delay caused some to cancel their orders.

D

■ On a separate sheet write the sentences below.
■ Underline the verbs and verb phrases.
■ Place parentheses around prepositional phrases.
■ Place a bracket above each infinitive or infinitive phrase, and label its use in the sentence.
■ Place a bracket above each gerund or gerund phrase, and label its use in the sentence.
■ Label all principal parts.

1. To watch was painful.

2. The best defense is to prepare.

3. He tried to run.

4. The children want us to take them to the beach.

5. To watch television too much is certainly unwise.

6. Her first stop was to cash her check.

7. My hardest chore was liking liver.

8. His highest ambition is to learn English.

9. Everyone tried to buy a copy.

10. Mrs. Gold enjoys riding her bicycle to the golf course.

11. Lighting the lanterns marked the festival's beginning.

12. We desire customers to pay in cash.

E

- On a separate sheet write the sentences below.
- Underline the verbs and verb phrases in each sentence.
- Place parentheses around prepositional phrases.
- Place a bracket above each verbal or verbal phrase (gerund or infinitive); label its use in the sentence.
- Label all principal parts.
- Punctuate where necessary.

1. Many are opposed to passing the bill consequently the legislators will probably postpone the voting.

2. The only recourse is to fight harder then the team's winning will not seem so impossible.

3. They asked him to dine with them however to do so would have meant his missing his plane.

4. Swimming bowling and dancing were some of the activities but most of the guests seemed disinterested.

5. After being advised of the very serious situation, she sent the museum a large check.

6. The judge ordered both to appear in court for questioning.

7. The instructor made learning physics very easy and I think her an exceptional teacher.

F

- On a separate sheet write the sentences below.
- Underline the verbs or verb phrases.
- Place parentheses around the prepositional phrases.
- Place a bracket above each verbal or verbal phrase; label its use in the sentence.
- Label all principal parts.
- Punctuate where necessary.

1. The packages were too large for sending in the regular mail therefore we required customers to return them personally.

2. The coach wanted me to practice daily for he thought the competition very keen.

3. My sister's plan has been to write type and mail the manuscript by February but she will not meet her deadline.

4. To escape meant our leaving the wounded behind and death for them would have been inevitable.

5. Some have been hoping for a transfer nevertheless I consider the possibility a remote one.

6. Learning to type will require much practice moreover to be good at shorthand will not be easy.

7. His final obstacle would be getting approval then all would be in readiness.

SKILL TEST

- ■ On a separate sheet write the sentences below.
- ■ Underline the verbs or verb phrases in each sentence.
- ■ Place parentheses around prepositional phrases.
- ■ Place a bracket above each verbal or verbal phrase; label its use in the sentence.
- ■ Label all principal parts.
- ■ Punctuate where necessary.

1. My taking Spanish has helped me with my English it has given me a better grasp of grammar.

2. Our original decision was to be in Boston for the conference however the weather has caused us to change our plans.

3. I am typing my final paper now.

4. They were adamant about paying for the dinner so we didn't argue the point.

5. To complete the test in the allotted time is quite difficult.

6. Everyone enjoyed working on the roadshow and all really tried to do their best.

7. The club required us to be present for the awards.

SKILL 4

Identifying Subordinate Clauses Used as Nouns

A *clause* (a group of words with a subject and verb) does not always express a complete thought.

```
      n pro(S)  AV   n(DO)
that   she   has  talent
```

Unlike a main clause that can stand alone as a complete sentence, a clause like the above is only a part of a sentence. Study the example below.

```
                n(S)           what?
        ┌───────────────────┐│
        │ n pro(S) AV  n(DO)││ LV    P Adj
That│  she   has talent│►is  obvious.
```

Any clause that does not express a complete thought is called a *subordinate clause* (a name that suggests that it is lower in rank than the main clause).

```
n pro(S) aux    AV
  I     am running ( for office. )◄──────── Main clause
      n pro(S) aux    AV
why    I     am running ( for office )◄──── Subordinate clause
```

Use the letters *n cl* to label a *noun clause.*

A subordinate clause can function as a single noun. Such a clause is called a *noun clause.* A noun clause can function as a subject. Study the example below.

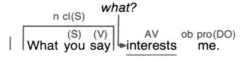

```
        n cl(S)    what?
     ┌──────────┐│
     │ (S)  (V) ││   AV      ob pro(DO)
│ │What you say│►interests    me.
```

A noun clause can function as a predicate nominative.

what?

n cl(PN)

d pro(S) LV (S) (V)
| | That is how my mother does it.

A noun clause can also function as a direct object.

what?

n cl(DO)

n pro(S) aux AV (S) (V)
They could tell which one was a fake.

A noun clause can function as an object of a preposition.

what?

n cl(OP)

n(S) LV P Adj (S) (V)
The school was proud (of what they did.)

Noun clauses usually begin with the following words:

Interrogative Adverbs	Pronouns
how	who (whoever)
when	whom (whomever)
where	whose
why	which (whichever)
	what (whatever)
	that

Often the word *that* is omitted before a noun clause.

n cl(DO)

n(S) AV (S) (V) (V)
Natalie said she could fix it.

A sentence that contains a noun clause is a <u>complex</u> sentence. A *complex* sentence contains a <u>main clause</u> (a clause that expresses a complete thought) and one or more <u>subordinate clauses</u> (clauses that do not express complete thoughts). Study the complex sentence below.

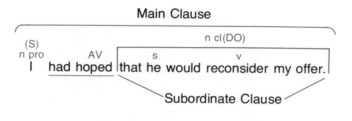

CHECKUP

Answer the following questions on a separate sheet of paper.

1. What name is given to those clauses that do not express a complete thought?
2. A clause that functions as a single noun is called what?
3. What two kinds of words begin such clauses?
4. Which introductory word is often omitted?
5. What is a complex sentence?

A

■ On a separate sheet complete the noun clauses in the brackets below by furnishing appropriate words.
■ If necessary, use the symbols to refer to the examples on pages 109–110.

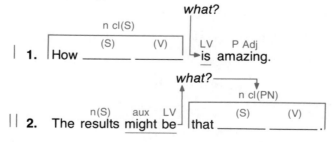

what? ⟶

n cl(DO)

n pro(S)　AV　　　　　　　(S)　　　(V)

☐ **3.**　I　want ⌐ whatever _____ _____ .

n cl(OP)

n(S)　aux　　AV　　p　　　(S)　　　(V)

☐ **4.**　Citizens are puzzled (about | which _____ _____ .)

B

■ Study the lists of words that begin noun clauses.
■ On a separate sheet of paper list the words using the letters below as clues.

Interrogative Adverbs

h __ __
w __ __ n
__ h __ r __
__ __ y

Pronouns

w __ o (__ ho __ v __ __)
w __ om (__ __ __ __ __ __ __ __)
w __ __ s __
__ h __ c __ (__ __ i __ h __ v __ __)
__ __ __ t (__ __ a __ e __ __ r)

t __ __ t

C

■ On a separate sheet write the sentences below.
■ Underline the verbs and verb phrases.
■ Place parentheses around prepositional phrases.
■ Place a bracket over each noun clause, and label its use in the sentence.
■ Indicate the subject (S) and verb (V) within the subordinate clause.
■ Label all other words.
■ If necessary, use the symbols to refer to the examples on pages 109–110.

☐ **1.** Everyone soon knew that the whole project was a mistake.

☐ **2.** You may donate the money to whichever charity you choose.

‖ **3.** The cause of the accident was that the brakes were wet.

| **4.** When the news will break is a matter of speculation.

☐ **5.** You may vote for whomever you choose.

‖ **6.** The truth is that I didn't study.

7. Several asked why I had not called.

8. Where they live is where the water is rising.

9. Our hopes depend on how well the community responds to our needs.

10. I realize I could win.

11. Who it is remains a secret.

12. Many didn't comprehend what had happened.

D

- On a separate sheet write the sentences below.
- Underline the verbs and verb phrases.
- Place parentheses around prepositional phrases.
- Place a bracket above each noun clause, and label its use in the sentence.
- Indicate the subject (S) and verb (V) within the subordinate clause.
- Place a bracket above each verbal or verbal phrase; label its use in the sentence.
- Label all other words.

1. What they have accomplished is a miracle.

noun clauses

2. The examiner can be whomever you choose.

3. The group decided that I should be the spokesperson.

4. We judged them by how each responded to the question.

5. Neither thought they were adequate.

6. Tatting is becoming a lost art.

7. My worst symptom is my coughing.

gerunds

8. I love dancing.

9. He gave practicing the guitar his every free moment.

10. Those failed by procrastinating too long.

11. Maria's very bad pitching lost us the game.

12. To be a good listener is a valuable talent.

infinitives

13. Our first task will be to find a reliable assistant.

14. Chris wants me to wash the car.

■ On a separate sheet write the sentences below.
■ Underline the verbs and verb phrases.
■ Place parentheses around prepositional phrases.
■ Place a bracket above each noun clause, and label its use in the sentence.
■ Indicate the subject (S) and verb (V) within the subordinate clause.
■ Place a bracket above each verbal or verbal phrase; label its use in the sentence.
■ Label all other words.

1. Whoever volunteers would be foolish.

2. To arrive on time is imperative.

3. The most reliable remedy for your bad grades is more studying.

4. Our playing in their field probably gives them the edge.

5. He instructed us thoroughly on how we should dress for the trip.

6. The impossible job will be to bring the two parties into agreement.

7. The color can be whatever you choose.

8. This month I won by selling the most.

9. The chairperson desires everyone to be seated.

10. Then these decided they would vote for me.

11. The professor deemed sculpturing the highest form of art.

12. Many haven't determined who is the best qualified.

SKILL TEST

■ On a separate sheet write the sentences below.
■ Underline the verbs and verb phrases.
■ Place parentheses around prepositional phrases.
■ Place a bracket above each noun clause, and label its use in the sentence.
■ Indicate the subject (S) and verb (V) within the subordinate clause.
■ Place a bracket above each verbal or verbal phrase; label its use in the sentence.
■ Label all other words.

1. Whoever volunteers would be foolish.

2. To arrive on time is imperative.

3. The most reliable remedy for your bad grades is more studying.

4. Our playing in their field probably gives them the edge.

5. He instructed us thoroughly on how we should dress for the trip.

6. The impossible job will be to bring the two parties into agreement.

7. The color can be whatever you choose.

8. This month I won by selling the most.

9. The chairperson desires everyone to be seated.

10. Then these decided they would vote for me.

CONCEPTS

Below is a list of labels representing the concepts that you have studied in this unit. As a review of words, phrases, and clauses used as nouns, look at each set of labels and try to recall the type of sentence each represents. If you have any difficulty, turn back to the appropriate section and review it before going further.

1. a. n(S)   __V__   (Complement).

    b. ⌈n(S) ger⌉   __V__   (Complement).

page 87

    c. ⌈n(S) ger phr⌉   __V__   (Complement).

page 95

n(S)

page 102   **d.** ⌐inf⌐   V   (Complement).

n(S)

page 102   **e.** ⌐inf phr⌐   V   (Complement).

n(S)

page 109   **f.** ⌐n cl(S) (V)⌐   V   (Complement).

    2.   **a.**   S   LV   n(PN).

n(PN)

page 87   **b.**   S   LV   ⌐ger .⌐

n(PN)

page 96   **c.**   S   LV   ⌐ger phr.⌐

n(PN)

page 103   **d.**   S   LV   ⌐inf .⌐

n(PN)

page 103   **e.**   S   LV   ⌐inf phr.⌐

n(PN)

page 110   **f.**   S   LV   ⌐n cl(S) (V) .⌐

    3.   **a.**   S   AV   n(DO).

n(DO)

page 88   **b.**   S   AV   ⌐ger .⌐

n(DO)

page 96   **c.**   S   AV   ⌐ger phr.⌐

n(DO)

page 103   **d.**   S   AV   ⌐inf .⌐

n(DO)

page 103   **e.**   S   AV   ⌐inf phr.⌐

n(DO)

page 110   **f.**   S   AV   ⌐n cl(S) (V).⌐

4. a. S   __AV__   n(IO)   n(DO).

page 88   **b.** S   __AV__   ⌈n(IO) ger⌉ n(DO).

5. a. S   __V__   (p n(OP)).

page 88   **b.** S   __V__   (p ⌈n(OP) ger⌉).

page 97   **c.** S   __V__   (p ⌈n(OP) ger phr⌉).

page 110   **d.** S   __V__   (p ⌈n(OP) n cl(S) (V)⌉).

REVIEW A

■ On a separate sheet write sentences to fit each formula in the preceding Concepts section.

■ If necessary, use the page references to refer to appropriate examples.

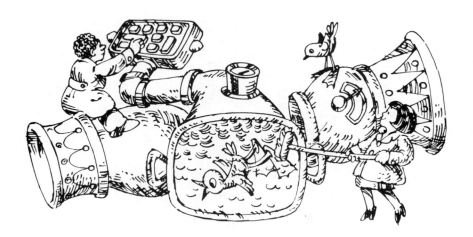

REVIEW B

■ On a separate sheet complete the following statements.

1. A verb ending in <u>ing</u> used as a <u>noun</u> is called a _____.

2. A gerund phrase includes a gerund and complements and modifiers that answer the following six questions: _____, _____, _____, _____, _____, _____.

3. A gerund phrase always begins with a _____.

4. A verb preceded by the preposition <u>to</u> constitutes an _____.

5. An infinitive phrase begins with an infinitive followed by _____ and _____ that answer questions _____, _____, _____, _____, _____, _____.

6. A noun or pronoun can precede an infinitive as part of an infinitive phrase only when the phrase follows an _____ _____ and serves as a _____ _____.

7. A subordinate clause is a group of words with a _____ and _____ that does _____ express a complete thought.

8. A complex sentence contains a _____ clause and one or more _____ clauses.

9. A sentence that contains a noun clause is a _____ sentence.

REVIEW C

■ On a separate sheet write the sentences below.
■ Label all words.

1. The salesperson gave us a sample.

2. I felt the alpaca fur.

3. The alpaca fur feels very soft.

4. Her room is her castle.

5. I believe him innocent.

6. She fussed about the delay.

7. We were abroad this summer.

8. They elected him secretary.

REVIEW D

■ On a separate sheet write the sentences below.
■ Underline the verb or verb phrase in each main clause.
■ Place parentheses around prepositional phrases.
■ Place a bracket above any verbal, verbal phrase, or clause used as a noun.
■ Label its use in the sentence.
■ Label all principal parts.
■ Punctuate where necessary.

1. Coming home early was an excellent decision for I really needed to get some sleep.

2. You push and I'll pull.

3. The guests are departing the orchestra is retiring and the clock is striking twelve.

4. Several police officers and medical personnel were on the scene.

5. These have caused us many complaints therefore I suggest that we reconsider their future production.

6. Closing this deal is essential we must not fail!

7. We love swimming bowling and fishing but neither of us likes to watch the spectator sports on television.

8. My brother thinks football dull but I think it the greatest sport of all.

REVIEW E

■ On a separate sheet write the sentences below.
■ Underline the verb or verb phrase in each main clause.
■ Place parentheses around prepositional phrases.
■ Place a bracket above any verbal, verbal phrase, or clause used as a noun.
■ Label its use in the sentence.
■ Label all principal parts.
■ Punctuate where necessary.

1. She is good at working with small children moreover dealing well with parents is another of her strong assets.

2. Now I must give preparing for my exams all of my time so my pleasures like sketching cooking and watching television unfortunately must wait.

3. My first objective in reading is to stay informed.

4. My problem was having a monkey for a pet.

5. We know that he is very capable what he has already accomplished for us makes this fact very obvious.

6. The boss wanted me to work late but to have done so would have meant my missing the concert.

7. Resigning now makes me the villain however my only hope of surviving is to get out now.

8. What we can do about the problem demands our first concern also another urgent matter is what caused the problem.

GRAMMAR

STEP-BY-STEP

UNIT W

Phrases and Clauses Used as Adjectives

UNIT IV

Phrases and Clauses Used as Adjectives

SKILL 1

Identifying Prepositional Phrases Used as Adjectives

Just as a simple adjective can modify a noun,

adj   n   adj   n
dark horse   weird noises

so also can a prepositional phrase. See below.

adj   n(S) LV   P Adj
The red-haired boy is handsome.

n(S)   prep phr-adj   LV   P Adj
The boy (with red hair) is handsome.

A prepositional phrase that is used as an adjective usually modifies the noun that precedes it.

A prepositional phrase used as an adjective responds to the questions *which* and *what kind of*. These questions are asked before the noun. See below.

which woman?

n(S)   prep phr-adj   LV   n(PN)
The woman (in the blue suit) is the top executive.

what kind of orchids?

n(S)   prep phr-adj   aux   AV
Orchids (of the palest green) were used.

123

Prepositional phrases used as adjectives can modify not only nouns used as subjects but also nouns used as predicate nominatives.

what kind of girl?

n pro(S) LV n(PN) prep phr-adj
She is a girl (with high ambitions.)

They modify nouns used as direct objects.

what kind of calf?

n pro(S) AV n(DO) prep phr-adj
He owns a calf (with a broken leg.)

They modify nouns used as indirect objects.

which athlete?

n pro(S) AV n(IO) prep phr-adj n(DO)
They awarded the athlete (from Georgia) the title.

They modify nouns used as objects of prepositions.

which books? *which wall?*

n(S) prep phr-adj prep phr-adj LV
The books (on the south wall) (of the library) are

n(PN)
biographies.

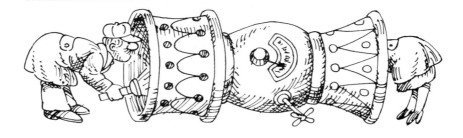

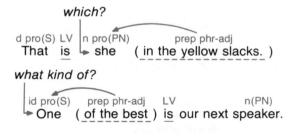

Prepositional phrases used as adjectives can also modify <u>pronouns</u>.

which?

d pro(S) LV |n pro(PN)   prep phr-adj
That   <u>is</u>   she   (<u>in the yellow slacks.</u>)

what kind of?

id pro(S)   prep phr-adj   LV   n(PN)
One   (<u>of the best</u>)   <u>is</u>   our next speaker.

CHECKUP

Answer the following questions on a sheet of paper.

1. Which noun does a prepositional phrase used as an adjective usually modify?
2. What other parts of speech can prepositional phrases used as adjectives modify?

A

■ On a separate sheet complete the following sentences by furnishing a prepositional phrase to modify the noun indicated.
■ Label the phrase appropriately.
■ Label the principal parts of each sentence.

which?

1. The puppy (_____) is really cute.

what kind of?

2. He is the new president (_____).

what kind of?

3. The newscaster is giving a report (_____).

which?

4. The landlord promised the couple (_____) a new lease.

which?   *what kind of?*

5. Victor bought the girl (_____) a box (_____).

which?

6. It is on the ▸table (___ ___).

which?

7. Bring me ▸those (___ ___).

which?   *which?*

▸(OP)

8. ▸Several (___ ___) (___ ___) thought the decision unwise.

B

■ On a separate sheet write the sentences below.
■ Underline the verb or verb phrase.
■ Place parentheses around prepositional phrases.
■ Draw a broken line beneath each phrase; label appropriately and draw an arrow to the noun or pronoun modified.
■ Label all principal parts.

EXAMPLE:

(S)
id pro   prep phr-adj   prep phr-adj   LV   n(PN)
Most (of the members) (of our club) are honor students.

1. This morning I'm taking my test in computer science.

2. Some of the essays have already been graded.

3. Her mother's friend is a person of unusual talents.

4. The visitors from Texas are generous.

5. The employees on our assembly line have really proven themselves dependable.

6. They voted the chairperson of our group next year's president.

7. The committee thought the projects on solar energy extremely worthwhile.

8. These are good ones for our demonstration.

9. We planned the rally before the game on Friday night.

10. My neighbor paid the boy across the street four dollars.

C

■ On a separate sheet number from 1 to 8.
■ Write the prepositional phrases used as adjectives in each sentence beside the corresponding number.
■ After each, write the noun or pronoun it modifies and the use of the noun or pronoun in the sentence.

EXAMPLE:

The comic on last night's special was an excellent imitator of the President.
(on last night's special)   comic (S)
(of the President)   imitator (PN)

1. The legislator classified the study on flood control in the Salt River Valley the top priority for this session.

2. The tourists from Mexico are very gracious.

An allotment is a planned distribution.

3. The ones in this allotment are poor specimens for our biology experiment.

4. They awarded the secretary of our class a full scholarship at Arizona State University.

5. My friend's sister is an engineer with several inventions in metal processing.

6. Several of the questions on the psychology test were very difficult.

7. Last week I took the exam in failure analysis.

8. The teacher asked the student in the back row a question concerning the geometry assignment.

SKILL TEST

■ On a separate sheet number from 1 to 6.
■ Write the prepositional phrases used as adjectives in each sentence beside the corresponding number.
■ After each, write the noun or pronoun it modifies and the use of the noun or pronoun in the sentence.

1. Then Congress sent the wife of the dead officer the country's highest award for bravery.

2. The heads of this company consider a degree in business indispensable.

3. Every network in the country announced the facts about the swindle and the names of the responsible individuals.

4. Last year she suddenly married a millionaire from a small town in Tennessee.

5. Unfortunately the fire was the work of some youths from our neighborhood.

6. A few of the debaters on our team are exceptionally gifted.

If something is *indispensable,* it is essential and absolutely necessary.

SKILL 2

Identifying Participles Used as Adjectives

A verb usually has four forms: <u>present</u>, <u>present participle</u>, <u>past</u>, and <u>past participle</u>. Study the chart below.

Present	**Present Participle**	**Past**	**Past Participle**
	aux ↓		aux ↓
I <u>sing</u>	I am sing(ing)	I <u>sang</u>	I have sung
	aux		aux
I <u>write</u>	I was writ(ing)	I <u>wrote</u>	I had writt(en)
	aux		aux
I <u>finish</u>	I was finish(ing)	I <u>finished</u>	I had finish(ed)

Note above that a participle is a form of a verb preceded by an auxiliary verb when used as the verb of a sentence. Note also that present participles always end in *ing.* Past participles frequently end in *ed* and *en.*

Use the abbreviation *prt* to label a *participle.*

Participles are sometimes verbals (verbs used as a different part of speech). They sometimes function as adjectives. Study the examples below.

adj(past prt) n(S) AV
The finished script <u>arrived</u> (on time.)

(S)
n pro aux AV   adj(present prt) n(OP)
We <u>were served</u> (by a singing waiter.)

(S)
n pro AV adj(past prt) n(DO)
I received a written reply.

IMPORTANT

Participles used as adjectives are never preceded by auxiliary verbs.

A participle used as a verb should not be confused with a participle used as a verbal. Note below.

(S)
n pro aux AV
He is living (in Puerto Rico.)

Living is preceded by an auxiliary and is the verb of the sentence.

(S)
n pro LV adj(prt) n(PN)
She is a living legend.

Living is not preceded by an auxiliary. It precedes a noun and is an adjective.

CHECKUP

Answer the following questions on a separate sheet of paper.

1. What are the names of the four common verb forms?
2. Which of the four forms, when used as verbs in sentences, are always preceded by auxiliary verbs?
3. What is characteristic of all present participles?
4. What are the frequent endings of past participles?
5. What is a verbal?
6. How can one distinguish between a participle used as a verb and a participle used as an adjective?

A

- On a separate sheet write the sentences below leaving a blank as indicated.
- Underline and label the verb or verb phrase.
- Use the verb of the sentence as an adjective placing it in the blank.
- Draw a broken line beneath each participle used as an adjective; label it appropriately and draw an arrow to the word it modifies.
- Label other principal parts of the sentence.

EXAMPLE:

The _____ car must be leased now.

adj(prt) n(S) aux aux AV
The leased car must be leased now.

1. Our _____ relatives will be visiting us soon.

2. This _____ beef was canned here.

3. The _____ forests have been burning constantly.

4. The _____ ball was moving rapidly.

5. Her much _____ question could not be avoided.

B

■ On a separate sheet write the sentences below.
■ Underline and label the verb or verb phrase.
■ Draw a broken line beneath each participle used as an adjective; label it appropriately and draw an arrow to the word it modifies.
■ Label other principal parts of the sentence.

1. Our one working model is functioning efficiently.

2. The newly elected representative is traveling abroad.

3. The finished scene has given the viewers a shocking experience.

4. The expected guest was a promising young poet.

5. The concealed pocket contained a guarded document.

C

■ On a separate sheet of paper, write the sentences below.
■ Underline and label the verb or verb phrase.
■ Draw a broken line beneath each participle used as an adjective; label appropriately and draw an arrow to the word it modifies.
■ Label other principal parts.

1. The village celebrated the engagement.

2. The celebrated scientist deemed our project very crucial.

3. The man delivered them some cleaning fluid.

4. They are cleaning the last container now.

5. The city has just repaved our street.

6. Our repaved street is a great improvement.

7. The dried leaves are everywhere.

8. My mother dried her glasses thoroughly.

9. The teacher is missing his stapler.

10. I saw the missing one this morning.

11. She is passing chemistry.

12. The passing bus honked its horn.

13. The newly painted building was very impressive.

14. Some students had painted the mural.

D

■ On a separate sheet number from 1 to 10.
■ Beside each number, list the participles and prepositional phrases used as adjectives in the corresponding sentence.
■ After each, write the noun or pronoun each modifies, and indicate the use of the noun or pronoun in the sentence.

EXAMPLE:

He is an experienced member of a disappearing act.
experienced   member (PN)
disappearing   act (OP)
(of a disappearing act)   member (PN)

1. Even the learned experts thought the Leaning Tower fascinating.

2. We established a fund for endangered species.

3. The somewhat puzzled detective considered the missing article a significant clue in the case.

An *emissary* is a messenger.

4. The dreaded emissary of the king brought the feared announcement about the heavier tax levy.

5. The abandoned site near the rapidly deteriorating dam in Orem Canyon is least desirable.

6. This stuffed owl by our most respected taxidermist is a prize winner.

7. They bought themselves a used typewriter.

8. The borrowed sanding machine sanded well.

9. The cooked ones at our last catered luncheon were not popular.

10. He sold them chopped broccoli, frozen peas, and mixed vegetables.

■ On a separate sheet number from 1 to 8.
■ Beside each number, list the participles and prepositional phrases used as adjectives found in the corresponding sentence.
■ After each, write the noun or pronoun it modifies and indicate the use of the noun or pronoun in the sentence.

1. The dancing bear from Borneo was unusual entertainment for the children.

2. Luis gave the injured raccoon fruit from his father's orchard and some water from the Fox River.

3. She considered the stuffed elk's head her most prized hunting trophy.

Decelerated means decreased in speed.

4. The newly hired instructor for the decelerated science classes thought the teaching assignment very difficult; nevertheless, he made himself a detailed plan of action and began.

5. The littered campus at Cortez was disgraceful, so the graduating class sponsored a carefully developed program for improvement.

6. Our stunned opponents stood speechless; our badly crippled and often trailing team had won.

7. The charred house fell, the flickering embers died, and the soothing rains began.

8. The stranded victims in the dense area of the mountain forest welcomed the dropped supplies.

■ On your paper write the reasons for the internal punctuation (commas and semicolons) in sentences 4, 5, 6, and 7.

SKILL TEST

■ On a separate sheet number from 1 to 5.
■ Beside each number, write the participles and prepositional phrases used as adjectives found in the corresponding sentence.
■ After each, write the noun or pronoun it modifies and indicate the use of the noun or pronoun in the sentence.

1. The demanded raise seemed unreasonable such increased wages would be a burden on the already weak economy.

2. They want a typed copy of the manuscript but someone from the advertising department has already sent them one.

3. The worried government officials thought the reduced prices of farm products a disturbing setback for the farmers moreover the newly released report on the economy showed inflation rising.

4. The conducted tours of the castle near Toronto are every hour consequently the members of your group should have no scheduling problem.

Unpalatable means not acceptable to the taste.

5. The burned cookies were tasteless the mashed sandwiches were unpalatable and the melted ice cream was completely worthless.

■ On your paper list the numbers of those sentences requiring internal punctuation.
■ After each number write each word in the sentence that should be followed by punctuation and the mark that should follow it.

REVIEW A

■ On a separate sheet number from 1 to 10.
■ Beside each number, write any phrase or clause used as a noun in the corresponding sentence.
■ After each phrase and clause, write its kind (gerund or infinitive phrase or noun clause) and its use in the sentence.

1. Turning this valve to the right releases the excess steam.

2. He soon learned whom he could trust.

3. The results can be achieved only by maintaining the solution at room temperature.

4. The next procedure will be to isolate the bacteria.

Designated
means indicated
or specified.

5. She designated learning Spanish her educational priority.

6. To win now is almost impossible.

7. The hardest job might be changing the public's attitude.

8. Whatever happens to us is totally unpredictable.

9. Our client wants to buy your house.

10. We received a letter concerning how the plan will work.

REVIEW B

■ On a separate sheet write the sentences below.
■ Underline the verb or verb phrase.
■ Place parentheses around prepositional phrases.
■ Place a bracket above any phrase (gerund or infinitive) or any clause used as a noun; label appropriately.
■ Draw a broken line beneath each participle and prepositional phrase used as an adjective.
■ Label appropriately and draw an arrow to the word each modifies.
■ Label all principal parts.

1. Reading these articles will reveal a more simplified solution to the problem.

2. The advanced class in chemistry needs to learn the new process.

3. The winning entry in the poster contest will depend entirely on who the judge is.

4. The burning ambition of her high school days was to perform in the Olympics.

5. Some of the leaders of the clubs gave the canned food drive their most dedicated efforts.

6. The unanswered question is how we should proceed from here.

7. To baste the meat is a required and rewarding step in the process.

8. The next calculated move will be distracting the enemy.

9. Everyone in my Spanish class wants me to bring my guitar to the party.

10. Traveling on the freeways is a frightening aspect of life in the city.

SKILL 3

Identifying and Punctuating Sentences Containing Participial Phrases

Note the endings that identify participles.

A participle used as an adjective can function alone or can be accompanied by other words. When a participle is accompanied by other words, a phrase is formed called a *participial phrase.* Study the examples below.

adj(prt)   n(S)   AV   n(DO)
The <u>shouting</u> spectators <u>ignored</u> the soft drizzle.

n(S)   prt phr-adj   AV   n(DO)
The spectators <u>shouting</u> (for victory) <u>ignored</u> the drizzle.

Note above that the participle alone precedes a noun; the participial phrase usually follows the noun it modifies.

Like gerunds and infinitives, participles become phrases when they are accompanied by complements and modifiers that respond to the six questions *who(m), what, how, when, where,* and *why.*

Participial phrases not only follow and modify subjects but also follow and modify <u>predicate nominatives</u>. See below.

n pro(S) LV   n(PN)   prt phr-adj
I   <u>am</u> a parent <u>concerned</u> (about children's safety.)

n pro(S) aux   LV   n(PN)   prt phr-adj
It   <u>will remain</u> a mission <u>clothed</u> (in secrecy.)

Participial phrases also modify <u>direct objects</u>.

n pro(S)   AV   n(DO)   prt phr-adj
He   has a <u>truck</u> <u>painted purple</u>.

n pro(S)   AV   n(DO)   prt phr-adj
I   <u>mailed</u> the <u>letter</u> <u>written yesterday</u>.

They also modify <u>indirect objects</u>.

n pro(S) AV   n(IO)   prt phr-adj   n(DO)
He   <u>sent</u> the <u>woman</u> <u>directing the drive</u> a large <u>donation</u>.

They also modify <u>object complements</u>.

n pro(S)   AV   ob pro(DO)   n(OC)   prt phr-adj
She   <u>thought</u>   you   a <u>genius</u> <u>wasting your life</u>.

Note the endings that identify participles.

Note the endings that identify participles.

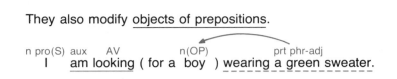

They also modify <u>objects of prepositions</u>.

n pro(S)   aux   AV   n(OP)   prt phr-adj
I   <u>am looking</u> (for a boy) <u>wearing a green sweater.</u>

Participial phrases also modify <u>pronouns</u>. See below.

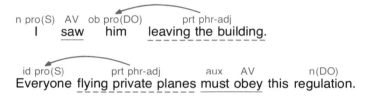

n pro(S) AV ob pro(DO)   prt phr-adj
I   <u>saw</u>   him   <u>leaving the building.</u>

id pro(S)   prt phr-adj   aux   AV   n(DO)
Everyone <u>flying private planes</u> <u>must obey</u> this regulation.

Sometimes a participial phrase does not follow the word that it modifies. In such a case the noun or pronoun modified is usually obvious. Note below.

n pro(S)   AV   prt phr-adj
She   <u>searched</u> <u>hoping for some clue.</u>

Sometimes when a sentence containing a participial phrase is read, a slight pause occurs before and after the phrase. When such a sentence is written, the pauses are indicated by <u>commas</u>.

Pauses usually occur before and after participial phrases that modify proper nouns (the capitalized names of specific people and places). Such phrases are separated from the rest of the sentence by <u>commas</u>. Study the examples below.

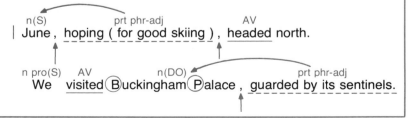

n(S)   prt phr-adj   AV
June , <u>hoping (for good skiing)</u> , <u>headed</u> north.

n pro(S)   AV   n(DO)   prt phr-adj
We   <u>visited</u> Buckingham Palace , <u>guarded by its sentinels.</u>

Pauses often occur before and after participial phrases that modify nouns preceded by possessives (possessive nouns, possessive pronouns, and possessive indefinite pronouns). Note below.

Note the endings that identify participles.

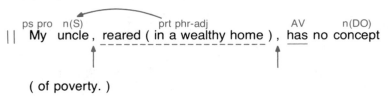

My uncle, reared (in a wealthy home), has no concept

(of poverty.)

Pauses also occur when a participial phrase modifies a noun preceded by several adjectives that specifically identify the noun. Note below.

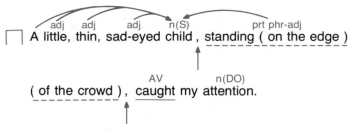

A little, thin, sad-eyed child, standing (on the edge)

(of the crowd), caught my attention.

There are exceptions to this rule. A writer has the freedom to indicate pauses before and after any participial phrase through the use of commas whenever such pauses contribute to the readability of the sentence.

Often the participial phrase is not separated from the rest of the sentence by commas. Note below.

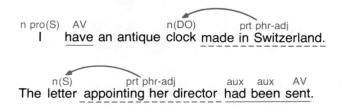

I have an antique clock made in Switzerland.

The letter appointing her director had been sent.

Note the endings that identify participles.

Although a participial phrase that modifies the subject of a sentence usually follows it, such a phrase can also precede it. Study the examples below.

n(S)　　　prt phr-adj　　　aux　　AV
Ed , tired after his hike , was sleeping (on the sofa.)

　　　prt phr-adj　　　n(S) aux　　AV
★ Tired after his hike , Ed was sleeping (on the sofa.)

　　　n(S)　prt phr-adj　aux　　AV　　　n(DO)
The plane flying low was scattering leaflets.

　　prt phr-adj　　　n(S)　aux　　AV　　　n(DO)
★ Flying low , the plane was scattering leaflets.

A comma always follows a participial phrase that precedes and modifies the subject. Study the examples (★) above.

A participial phrase that precedes the subject <u>must</u> modify it. When such a phrase does not modify the subject, the meaning of the sentence is usually unclear. Note below.

　　　prt phr-adj　　　　　　?　n(S)　　AV
Driving through the country, spotted cows grazed peacefully.

Phrases like the above are called *dangling participial phrases* because there is no noun or pronoun to which the phrase refers. Sentences with such phrases can be corrected by placing a noun or pronoun in the sentence that the phrase can modify. Note below.

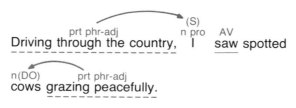

　　　　　　　　　　　　　　(S)
　　prt phr-adj　　　　　　n pro　AV
Driving through the country, I saw spotted

n(DO)　　　prt phr-adj
cows grazing peacefully.

Note the endings
that identify
participles.

A participial phrase is <u>misplaced</u> when it is located near a
noun other than the one it modifies. Study the examples.

n(S) AV   n(DO)?   prt phr-adj
The boy <u>saw</u> the accident <u>walking to school.</u>   Wrong

n(S)   prt phr-adj   AV   n(DO)
The boy <u>walking to school</u> <u>saw</u> the accident.   Correct

prt phr-adj   n(S) AV   n(DO)
<u>Walking to school</u>, the boy <u>saw</u> the accident.   Correct

prt phr-adj   ? ✕ n pro(S)   AV
<u>Cooked over an open fire</u>,   I   especially <u>enjoy</u>

n(DO)
fried fish.   Wrong

prt phr-adj   n(S) LV
<u>Cooked over an open fire</u>, fried fish <u>is</u> especially

P Adj
enjoyable.   Correct

n pro(S)   AV   n(DO)   prt phr-adj
I   especially <u>enjoy</u> fried fish <u>cooked over an open fire.</u>

Correct

A single noun or pronoun can be modified by a variety of
adjectives, words, and phrases. Study the example below.

adj(prt) n(S) prep phr-adj   prt phr-adj
The <u>shipping clerk</u> (<u>at the store</u>), <u>wearied (by the hassles)</u>

cj   prt phr-adj
(<u>of the day</u>) but <u>soothed (by the prospects)</u>

AV   adj(prt)   n(DO)
(<u>of a quiet weekend</u>), <u>locked</u> the <u>battered</u> office door.

⊠ Note above that when a noun has a variety of modifiers
(single words and phrases) and the participial phrase
cannot immediately follow the noun it modifies, it is
separated from the rest of the sentence by commas.

CHECKUP

Answer the following questions on a separate sheet of paper.

1. What is the usual position of a participial phrase in relation to the word it modifies?
2. What two parts of speech can participial phrases modify?
3. Under what four circumstances are commas used to separate a participial phrase from the rest of the sentence?
4. Which noun or pronoun in a sentence can be followed or preceded by the participial phrase that modifies it?
5. Must a participial phrase that precedes a subject always be separated from the rest of the sentence by a comma?
6. What is a dangling participial phrase?
7. What is a misplaced participial phrase?
8. What six questions does one ask to find the complements and modifiers that accompany a participle in a participial phrase?
9. What endings identify participles?

■ On a separate sheet number from 1 to 10.
■ Write the participial phrase found in each sentence beside the corresponding number.
■ After each, write the noun or pronoun it modifies and the use of the noun or pronoun in the sentence.

1. I have just finished *Cry, the Beloved Country,* written about the racial problems in South Africa.

2. The saleswoman left slamming the door behind her.

3. The weary, untrained, but determined farmers, pausing only moments to reload, continued their pursuit.

4. I saw them waiting on the steps of the library.

5. Mr. Green was a mayor trained in every aspect of leadership.

6. My sister, jogging past the school this afternoon, saw the smoke escaping from a front window.

7. Collected by a service organization at the high school, the money will be a boon to the school for the blind.

8. His acquaintances found him a ruthless man of the world, obsessed with a desire for money.

9. The officer gave the woman driving the pickup the ticket.

10. Bored by the discussion, I left the meeting early.

■ On your paper write the reasons for the internal punctuation in sentences 1, 3, 6, 7, and 8. If necessary, use the symbols before each sentence to refer to examples given on previous pages.

B

■ On a separate sheet number from 1 to 10.
■ Write the prepositional phrases (not found in participial phrases) and the participial phrases in each sentence beside the corresponding number.
■ After each, write the noun or pronoun it modifies and the use of the noun or pronoun in the sentence.

1. The church-sponsored summer tours of Europe organized especially for seminary students will last six weeks.

2. Today the restaurant is serving shrimp cooked creole style.

3. Pat's convertible bought three months ago is for sale.

4. I gave a secretary working in your office a message reminding you of our meeting.

5. A financial advisor to our firm considers it a good investment designed particularly for people of middle income.

6. A doctor of psychology had been counseling the wealthy and successful woman depressed about her relationship with her employees.

7. Everybody averaging ninety percent does not take a final exam in Spanish.

8. Training for the Olympics several of our athletes have temporarily discontinued their studies.

9. The movie critics writing in today's paper have given *Superman* starring Christopher Reeve a high rating on special effects.

10. The master of ceremonies hired by our committee did not arrive.

■ On your paper list the numbers of those sentences that need internal punctuation. (There are five.)
■ Beside each number write the word(s) in the sentence that should be followed by commas.
■ Be prepared to justify your use of commas.

On a sheet of paper write the sentences below. Label the principal parts in each.

Draw a broken line under each prepositional phrase (not found in a participial phrase) and each participial phrase; label each appropriately and draw an arrow to the word modified.

Punctuate where necessary.

1. A high school basketball team from Indianapolis playing in the state tournament broke the high scoring record.

2. Passersby watching the big cranes at work were fascinated.

3. The Senator speaking about the energy problem made a strong conservation plea.

4. My stepmother learning of her father's serious condition phoned the hospital immediately.

5. Moon Valley High School opening its doors ten years ago has become an institution of excellent reputation.

Rewrite each sentence in Drill C placing the participial phrase before the subject.

Draw an arrow from the phrase to the word modified.

Place commas where needed.

E

Complete each sentence below by adding a participial phrase.

Draw a broken line under each participial phrase; label appropriately and draw an arrow to the noun or pronoun modified.

Be prepared to give the reasons for the use of commas in sentences 1 and 6.

1. My brother, _____, was extremely nervous.

2. I noticed her _____.

3. Cancer is a disease _____.

4. The clerk sent a company _____ the damaged part.

5. We voted for the amendment _____.

6. _____, the watch needed repair.

F

■ On a separate sheet rewrite each sentence below correcting the misplaced or dangling participial phrase.
■ Place a broken line beneath each phrase.
■ Draw an arrow from each participial phrase to the word modified.
■ Place commas where necessary.

1. Locked in cages, we felt sorry for the abandoned animals.

2. The plane hit the steeple flying too low.

3. Skating on the lake, the day was exceptionally fun.

4. Arriving late for school, the teacher sent me to the office.

5. The dog frightened the boy barking furiously.

6. Taking too long for breakfast, the bus left me.

7. The child was struck by a car playing in the street.

8. Sitting on a park bench, my eye caught a most unusual sight.

G

■ On a separate sheet of paper rewrite each pair of sentences below into a single sentence by changing the second into a participial phrase and placing it near the noun that it modifies in the first sentence.
■ Punctuate where necessary.

1. He saw a beautiful, busy, red-crowned woodpecker.
   It was sitting on a branch outside his window.

2. My cousin is playing on a soccer team.
   The team is sponsored by the Lions Club.

3. Her mother quickly called him.
   She was hoping to catch the doctor at his office.

4. The judges gave the poem an award.
   The poem was written by my brother.

5. I saw it.
   It was lying on the dining room table.

■ On a separate sheet number from 1 to 5.
■ Beside each number, write the prepositional phrases (not found in participial phrases), and participial phrases used as adjectives in the corresponding sentence.
■ After each, write the noun or pronoun it modifies and the use of the noun or pronoun in the sentence.

1. The scene from the top of the mountain was one defying all description.

2. The last series of lectures on the uses of solar energy given by the professor at Purdue were extremely informative.

3. A snarling dog running down our street gave our mail carrier driving by in an open vehicle a terrible scare.

4. Deciding on an exotic menu the planning committee for the studio's golden anniversary celebration hired an experienced caterer from one of the best hotels.

5. The group leaving at eight o'clock will visit Sears Tower located about twenty miles from here.

■ On your paper list the numbers of those sentences that need internal punctuation.
■ Beside each number, write the word(s) in the sentence that should be followed by commas.

SKILL TEST

■ On a separate sheet number from 1 to 5.
■ Beside each number, write the prepositional phrases (not found in participial phrases), and participial phrases used as adjectives in the corresponding sentence.
■ After each, write the noun or pronoun it modifies and the use of each in the sentence.

1. The one lying on the ledge is a beautiful creature with unusual markings.

2. Stolen from the vault last week the marked money has been recovered.

3. The old, haunted house on Sycamore Street struck by lightning in last night's storm was totally destroyed.

4. The tiring but persistent detective finally captured the thief trying to catch a plane for South America.

5. The covered body resting on the stretcher was his neighbor's son burned beyond recognition.

■ On your paper number again from 1 to 5.
■ Beside each number, write the word(s) in each sentence that should be followed by a comma.

REVIEW

■ On a separate sheet number from 1 to 5.
■ Beside each number, write the prepositional phrases (not found in participial phrases), and participial phrases used as adjectives in the corresponding sentence.
■ After each, write the noun or pronoun it modifies and the use of each in the sentence.

1. Digging in Palestine an archaeologist found a sealed jar containing ancient scrolls and scientists deem this discovery an important one.

2. The person making the decision is one of the vice-presidents of the company however each of the managers of the divisions has some input.

3. Our negotiating committee representing over five thousand teachers gave the newly convened legislators a list of our proposals for the improvement of education in our state.

4. Assigned by the director one of the best men in the Bureau is heading the investigation into wiretapping suspected of several well-known officials.

5. We find her an educated woman of superior intelligence having considerable experience in her field she will be an excellent chief of research.

■ On your paper number again from 1 to 5.
■ Beside each number write the word(s), if any, in each sentence that should be followed by a mark of punctuation.
■ After each word write the appropriate mark.

SKILL 4

Identifying Infinitives and Infinitive Phrases Used as Adjectives

Infinitives also serve as adjectives when they follow and modify nouns. As other adjectives, they tell *which* and *what kind of* about the nouns that precede them. Study the examples below.

which?

n(S)   inf-adj   LV P Adv
The time to begin is now.

what kind of?

n(S) aux   AV   p   n(OP)   inf-adj
Mario was looking (for an excuse) to call.

Infinitive phrases (infinitives followed by complements that respond to the questions *who(m)* or *what* or modifiers that respond to the questions *how, when, where,* or *why*) can also serve as adjectives. Such phrases, like the simple infinitive, can follow and modify nouns or pronouns.

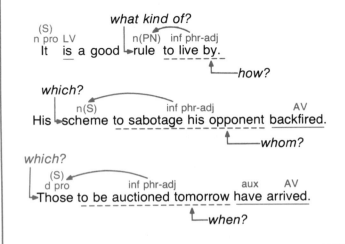

what kind of?

(S)
n pro LV   n(PN) inf phr-adj
It is a good rule to live by.

—how?

which?

n(S)   inf phr-adj   AV
His scheme to sabotage his opponent backfired.

—whom?

which?

(S)
d pro   inf phr-adj   aux   AV
Those to be auctioned tomorrow have arrived.

—when?

CHECKUP

Answer the following questions on a separate sheet.

1. What two questions do infinitives and infinitive phrases answer about the nouns they modify?
2. What is the position of the infinitive or the infinitive phrase in relation to the noun or pronoun it modifies?
3. What questions does one ask to find all complements and modifiers that belong in an infinitive phrase?

A

■ On a separate sheet complete each sentence below by furnishing an infinitive phrase. (Ask the appropriate questions before the noun that precedes each phrase.)

■ Place a broken line beneath each phrase; label it appropriately and draw an arrow to the noun or pronoun it modifies.

■ Label all principal parts.

EXAMPLE:

n pro(S) AV   n(DO)   inf phr-adj
She   has the talent to become a great teacher.

1. He always finds a way to _ _ _ _ _ _ _ .
2. Our plans to _ _ _ _ _ _ _ are exciting.
3. We voted her the woman to _ _ _ _ _ _ _ .
4. The books to _ _ _ _ _ _ _ will be delivered soon.
5. This year the team to _ _ _ _ _ _ _ is the Dodgers.
6. The trust fund provided them a way to _ _ _ _ _ _ _ .

B

■ On a separate sheet number from 1 to 6.

■ Beside each number, write the infinitive phrase(s) used as an adjective in the corresponding sentence.

■ After each, write the noun or pronoun it modifies and the use of the noun or pronoun in the sentence.

1. The generals devised a brilliant plan to end the war.
2. These are the ones to send to St. Louis.

3. Our ride to see the holiday decorations was very memorable.

4. Several thought your decision to sell these a serious mistake.

5. They bought a large order of food to go.

6. The cheapest place to buy clothes isn't always the best place to buy them.

C

■ Review infinitive phrases used as nouns by writing on your paper beside the corresponding number, the phrase in each sentence below and its use **(S, PN, DO).**

1. I plan to return on Sunday.

2. To sing at the Met is my greatest ambition.

3. My fear is to forget my lines on opening night.

4. The professor urged me to study more.

5. His last official act had been to pardon several criminals.

D

■ On your paper number from 1 to 10.
■ Beside each number, write the infinitive or infinitive phrase in the corresponding sentence.
■ If the phrase serves as an adjective, write the noun or pronoun it modifies and the function of the noun or pronoun.
■ If the phrase serves as a noun, identify its function as **S, PN,** or **DO.**

1. Atlanta is a fascinating place to visit.

2. To visit Atlanta someday would be fabulous.

3. My favorite entertainment is to watch a good baseball game.

4. The team to watch this year is the Chicago Cubs.

5. She expects to beat her opponent in the first match.

6. My professor discovered a system to beat the stock market.

7. The advisor gave the recommendations to be sent to the President her careful consideration.

8. To speak well is a valuable asset.

9. His desire for a chance to speak was refused.

10. The girl did not want to be sent to the principal.

E

■ On your paper number from 1–10.
■ Beside each number, list the phrases (all that are not included in other phrases) that serve as adjectives.
■ After each phrase identify the kind (prepositional, participial, or infinitive), the noun or pronoun it modifies, and the function of the word modified.

1. Determined to help we sent him money to be used for his medical expenses.

2. The amendment blocked during these debates will be reintroduced next session.

3. The best movie to see this weekend is at the Biograph.

4. The music teachers at Northwestern are several of the best artists in our area.

5. The workers hurriedly repaired the bridge weakened by the flood.

6. Her son waiting to see the doctor suddenly became very agitated.

7. Maria is a good person to handle this situation.

8. Mr. Shimoto trying to find a tutor for his son called the counselor.

9. A woman with an excessive desire to get rich often neglects things of greater value.

10. This short humorous scene by William Shakespeare suggested by Mr. Lopez would be the logical one to do first.

■ On your paper list the numbers of those sentences that need internal punctuation.
■ Beside each number, write the word(s) in the sentence that should be followed by commas.

SKILL TEST

■ On your paper number from 1 to 5.

■ Beside each number, list the phrases (all that are not included in other phrases) that serve as adjectives.

■ After each phrase, write its kind (prepositional, participial, or infinitive), the noun or pronoun it modifies, and the function of the word modified.

1. The most knowledgeable person to ask about your tax problem would be someone specializing in corporate taxes.

2. Later I saw the short man with the blonde mustache seated in the lobby of our hotel.

3. The officer in charge allowed the woman caught at the scene an opportunity to call her lawyer.

4. Your property in New Mexico located on the golf course is the best kind to own.

5. Made last December our plans to go abroad had then seemed feasible.

■ On your paper list the numbers of those sentences that need internal punctuation.

■ Beside each number write the word(s) in the sentence that should be followed by commas.

SKILL 5

Identifying and Punctuating Sentences Containing Adjective Clauses

A subordinate clause may be used not only as a noun but also as an adjective. When a subordinate clause follows and modifies a noun or a pronoun, it is called an adjective clause. Note below.

Subordinate Clause   that   I   <u>lost</u> last spring
(n pro — (S), AV above "that I lost")

Adjective Clause   The wallet <u>that I lost last spring</u>
<u>was returned</u>.
(n(S), adj cl, s v, aux AV labels)

Remember that a subordinate clause contains a subject and a verb; however, unlike a main clause it does not express a complete thought. Study the subordinate clauses below.

whom   I   <u>saw</u> (at the play)
(n pro, (S), AV)

that she <u>had bought</u> (on sale)
(n pro, (S), aux AV)

which <u>were left</u> (on the bus)
(pro, (S), aux AV)

Adjective clauses like the above should never be separated from a main clause. Used alone they are called sentence *fragments*.

An adjective clause can modify any <u>noun</u> in a sentence.
It can modify the <u>subject</u>. See below.

adj cl

n(S)   s   v   AV

| The foreman who works the night shift quit.

An adjective clause can modify the <u>predicate nominative</u>.

adj cl

(S)
n pro LV   n(PN)   s   v

|| He is the man who built our home.

An adjective clause can modify the <u>direct</u> or <u>indirect object</u>.

adj cl

(S)
n pro AV   n(DO) s   v

I hit the ball that went over the fence.

adj cl

n(S)   AV   n(IO)   s   v   n(DO)

The agency gave the woman who bought it a guarantee.

An adjective clause can modify the <u>object complement</u>.

adj cl

(S)   (DO)   =
n pro   AV   ob pro n(OC)   s   v

They consider him a scoundrel that should be exposed.

An adjective clause can modify the <u>object of the</u>
<u>preposition</u>.

adj cl

(S)
n pro AV   n(DO)   p   n(OP) s   v

I saw the girl (in the car) that had no license plates.

An adjective clause can modify a <u>pronoun</u>.

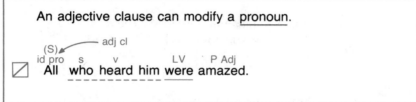

```
                    ── adj cl
     (S)
     id pro  s    v          LV    P Adj
☑    All  who heard him  were  amazed.
```

Prepositions sometimes precede the adjective clause.
Such prepositions are part of the clause. See below.

```
                        ── adj cl
       n(S)     p    s     v      aux   LV
☒  The neighbor to whom he had written  had moved.
```

```
     (S)
     n pro  aux   AV      n(OP)   p     s              v
     It   was placed ( in a cage ) from which it could not escape.
                                   ── adj cl
```

IMPORTANT

Read the previous sentences containing adjective clauses omitting the subordinate clauses. Note that when an adjective clause is omitted from a sentence, a main clause remains.

When a noun in a sentence is preceded by several modifiers that specifically identify it, an adjective clause that follows usually adds <u>extra</u> or <u>nonessential information</u>. Such a clause is separated from the main clause by commas.* Study the example below.

```
                                    ── adj cl
                          n(S)      s    v
◯  The little, red, wooden wagon , which was usually in the yard ,
       ↑    ↑      ↑      ↑
       identifying modifiers                nonessential

   aux      AV
   had disappeared.
```

*There are exceptions to this rule. A writer has the freedom to indicate pauses before and after any adjective clause through the use of commas whenever such pauses contribute to the readability of the sentence.

An adjective clause that follows a proper noun is also
considered nonessential and is therefore separated from
the main clause by commas. See below.

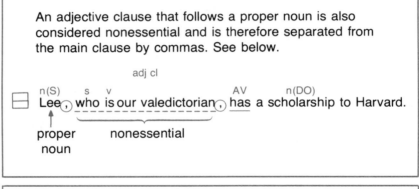

Whenever nouns are preceded by possessives (my,
everyone's, Pat's), adjective clauses that follow are
considered nonessential. Commas separate them from the
main clause.

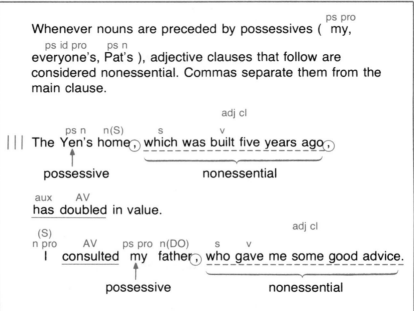

When a noun has a variety of modifiers (single words and
phrases) and the adjective clause cannot immediately
follow the noun it modifies, it is separated from the rest of
the sentence by commas.

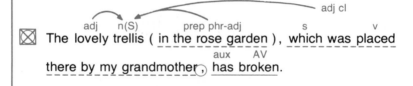

Adjective clauses that follow nouns not preceded by identifying modifiers are usually <u>essential</u> in completing the meaning of the sentence. They are not separated from the main clause by commas.

                                  adj cl

(S)
n pro LV   n(PN)   s   v
✉ She is a woman whom I admire.

                         adj cl

       n(S)   s   v   aux   AV
The book that you loaned me has disappeared.

All adjective clauses that begin with the pronoun *that* are considered essential. No commas are necessary.

                  adj cl

       n(S)   s   v   LV   P Adj
○ The children that attend are well behaved.
               ↑

                         adj cl

     n(S)   AV   n(DO) s   v
My neighbor has a cat that howls all night.
                       ↑

Words that usually introduce adjective clauses are the following:

	who	which
that	whom	when
	whose	where

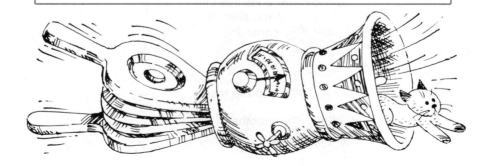

CHECKUP

Answer the following questions on a separate sheet of paper.

1. When does a subordinate clause serve as an adjective clause?
2. How does a subordinate clause differ from a main clause?
3. Under what four circumstances are adjective clauses separated by commas from main clauses?
4. Under what two circumstances are adjective clauses not separated by commas from main clauses?

■ On a separate sheet number from 1 to 16.
■ Read each group of words below carefully; then beside the corresponding number, write **sentence—main clause** if the group of words expresses a complete thought.
■ Write **fragment—subordinate clause** if the group of words does not express a complete thought.

1. Which he could remember clearly.
2. The officer listened intently to her story.
3. First we had to build a fire.
4. After the performance she left hurriedly.
5. Where the plants are shaded in the afternoon.
6. Last night the rain flooded our street.
7. In the spring when the air is full of pollen.
8. Then I will move to amend the motion.
9. When the package was brought to the front desk.
10. One of the tools of the poet is figurative language.
11. Which seemed to kill her appetite.
12. Who prides himself on his persuasive ability.
13. That served several terms each.
14. There had been a shrill whistle before the crash.
15. Whom they were not able to conquer.
16. The runners plodded over the final stretch.

B

- On a separate sheet of paper, write sentences to follow the directions given below.
- Label the subject and verb in all clauses.
- If necessary, use the symbols to refer to the examples given on the preceding pages.

1. Write a sentence with an adjective clause modifying the subject of the main clause.

2. Write a sentence with an adjective clause modifying a predicate nominative in the main clause.

3. Write a sentence with an adjective clause modifying a direct object in the main clause.

4. Write a sentence with an adjective clause modifying an indirect object in the main clause.

5. Write a sentence with an adjective clause modifying an object complement.

6. Write a sentence with an adjective clause modifying an object of a preposition.

7. Write a sentence with an adjective clause modifying a pronoun in the main clause.

C

- On your paper number from 1 to 8.
- Beside the corresponding number, write the adjective clause found in each sentence; identify the subject and the verb.
- After each clause, write the noun or pronoun it modifies and the use of the noun or pronoun in the sentence.

1. The committee chose a place where the delegates could have an easy access to a golf course.

2. The deaths of the two brilliant, young, aerospace scientists, who worked with my mother, are being investigated.

3. The damaged ones are some that I bought at an auction.

4. The teacher gave Rodney and Elizabeth, who had deliberately missed the test, a different one that was much more difficult.

5. The copy machine in the teachers' lounge, which has been used constantly all year, appears very reliable.

6. The coach considered him a player whose vanity sometimes interfered with his performance.

7. Our personnel department, to whom she has sent her resume, seems interested.

8. This is the best model we make.

■ On your paper write the reasons for the internal punctuation in sentences 2, 4, 5, and 7. If necessary use the symbols to refer to the examples given on the preceding pages.

D

■ On your paper number from 1 to 8.
■ Beside each number, write the adjective clause found in the corresponding sentence; identify the subject and the verb.
■ After each clause write the noun or pronoun it modifies and the use of the noun or pronoun in the sentence.

1. Tim Sanchez who was offered several scholarships will play football here.

2. All girls whom the coaches notified should be at practice this afternoon.

3. My father and uncle are members of the Lions Club which sponsors many worthwhile projects.

4. She remembered the tall, majestic but dying cottonwood which had provided shade for her childhood games.

5. Only customers that have an account with us are eligible.

6. The new shortstop on the Ranger team who hit the home run was injured on the play.

7. This species is one that is peculiar to North America alone.

8. We like her new receptionist who is not only efficient but also pleasant.

■ On your paper list the numbers of those sentences that need internal punctuation. (There are five.)
■ Beside each number write the word(s) in the sentence that should be followed by commas.

■ On your paper number from 1 to 8.
■ Beside each number, list the phrases and clauses in the corresponding sentence that serve as adjectives.
■ After each clause or phrase listed, identify its kind (prepositional, participial, or infinitive phrase or adjective clause).
■ Write the noun or pronoun each modifies and the use of the noun or pronoun in the sentence.

1. *Star Wars* which is a science fiction film is one that I really enjoyed.

2. The best shampoo to use is that in the white bottle with a blue label.

3. My aunt approaching her eightieth birthday knew the man who served as the town's first sheriff.

4. Believing that she could win she invested everything she had.

5. A dealer in New York sold him this rare, beautiful, and excellently preserved copy which was published in 1754.

6. Placing the package on the doorstep the stranger hurriedly entered a dark-colored car that was waiting.

7. The best answer to give under these circumstances is your refusal to negotiate.

8. The leaders of the gangs must take the responsibility for this tragedy.

■ On your paper list the numbers of those sentences that need internal punctuation.
■ Beside each number write the word(s) in the sentence that should be followed by commas.

SKILL TEST

■ On your paper number from 1 to 6.
■ Beside each number, list the phrases and clauses in the corresponding sentence that serve as adjectives.
■ After each modifier listed, identify its kind (prepositional, participial, or infinitive phrase or adjective clause).
■ Write also the noun or pronoun each modifies and the use of each in the sentence.

1. The person honored here tonight is a very beautiful, vivacious, and talented girl who has made herself a place in show business.

2. The ad which we placed in the Sunday paper has brought us excellent sales that will remove our deficit.

3. Wearied by the ordeal he sat thinking of happier days.

4. The thrill of victory at the Olympics was a moment to be treasured forever.

5. His sister's record established during her high school years has never been broken.

6. First the notice to report reached Jeff who then phoned me.

■ On your paper list the numbers of those sentences that need internal punctuation.
■ Beside each number write the word(s) in the sentence that should be followed by commas.

REVIEW A

■ On a separate sheet number from 1 to 10.
■ Beside each number, write any phrase (gerund or infinitive) or clause used as a noun.
■ After each phrase and clause, identify its use in the sentence.

1. Listening to the Sunday concert was the usual activity for entertaining oneself.

2. Her father needs her to help with the yardwork.

3. The donation can be given to whatever charity you designate.

4. The crew wanted to break their previous record.

5. To offend our sponsors in any way would be unforgivable.

6. His frequent diversion was practicing his fast ball against the side of the building.

7. They could guess what we were thinking.

8. Whichever you choose will be fine with me.

9. My advice would be to apply at several other places.

10. The assembly line workers enjoyed dressing up on Sunday.

REVIEW B

■ On your paper beside each number, write the subordinate clause found in the corresponding sentence below.

■ After each adjective clause, write the noun or pronoun it modifies and the function of each in the sentence.

■ After each noun clause, identify its function in the sentence **(S, PN, DO, OP).**

1. Scarlett's Plantation is a place where one can enjoy a relaxed Southern atmosphere.

2. The mystery is how they can live on so little money.

3. Each night you must deposit the money that you collect at the box office.

4. Those enthusiastic, hardworking students from the university, who joined in the cleanup after the flood, were a pleasant group to work with.

5. Several saw who did it.

6. What we can do tomorrow will depend on the weather.

7. The books that were thrown in the pool must be replaced.

8. Your suggestion about when we should begin our advertising is a good one.

SKILL 6

Identifying Appositives and Appositive Phrases

A noun can also be modified by an appositive. An *appositive* is a noun that follows and renames or identifies another noun. Study the sentences below.

Use the letters *app* to label an *appositive*.

```
  (S)
  n pro  LV   P Adj    p      n(OP)      app-adj
| She  was proud ( of her trade ), carpentry.
```

```
                    n(S)        app-adj       AV       n(DO)
  Our team captain, Norma Pappas, broke her  leg.
```

In an appositive phrase, the noun that follows and renames can be preceded by its own modifiers. Note below.

```
   (S)       (IO)                         app phr-adj
   n pro  AV  ob pro  n(DO) adj  adj   n adj
|| He  gave  her   a  gift,  a lovely pearl necklace.
                                ↑       ↑      ↑
                               modifiers
```

The noun in an appositive phrase can also be modified by phrases and clauses. See below.

app phr-adj
n(S)   AV   n(DO)
☐ Roy Donetti, a driver (with steel nerves), took chances.

prepositional phrase-adjective

app phr-adj
n(S)   s   v   AV
☐ Roy Donetti, a driver who had steel nerves, died.

adjective clause

app phr-adj
n(S)   AV
▧ Roy Donetti, a driver admired by thousands, died.

participial phrase-adjective

app phr-adj
n(S)   AV
▨ Roy Donetti, the man to be buried today, died (in a race).

infinitive phrase-adjective

An appositive phrase is always separated from the rest of the sentence by commas. (Note above.) However, when a simple appositive (one word) does not interrupt the flow of the sentence, no commas are necessary. Note below.

n(S)   app-adj   aux   AV
▤ My cousin Veronica is coming this summer.

> An appositive phrase can also consist of a pronoun accompanied by modifiers. Note below.
>
> app phr-adj
>
> n(S) id pro   prep phr-adj   s   v   AV
> Dad, <u>one (of the men) who originated the project,</u> <u>quit</u>.
>
> app phr-adj
>
> n(S)   d pro   prep phr-adj   aux   AV
> Several students, <u>those (with top grades),</u> <u>were placed</u> in a seminar.

CHECKUP

Answer the following questions on a separate sheet of paper.

1. What is an appositive?
2. What is an appositive phrase?
3. What are the various structures that can accompany an appositive in an appositive phrase?
4. What punctuation is usually required in sentences containing appositives or appositive phrases?
5. When do appositives not necessitate additional punctuation?
6. Besides the noun, what part of speech accompanied by modifiers can serve as an appositive phrase?

A

■ On a separate sheet complete the sentences below by furnishing the word or phrase indicated.
■ If necessary, use the symbols to refer to examples on the preceding pages.

app-adj

n(S)   AV   n(DO)
1. The Spanish teacher, _ _ _ _ _ _ _, <u>speaks</u> three languages.

app phr-adj

n(S)   n   LV   P Adj
2. The gift, _ _ _ _ _ _ _ _ _ _ _ _ _ _ _ _ _ _ _ _ _, <u>was</u> exquisite.

modifiers

app phr-adj

n(S)   n   prep phr-adj   LV   P Adj
3. The gift, _ _ _ _ _ _ _ _ _ _ _ _ _ _ (_ _ _ _ _ _ _), <u>was</u> exquisite.

app phr-adj

n(S)   n   adj cl   LV P Adj

☐ **4.** The gift, _____ _____ _____, **was** exquisite.

app phr-adj

n(S)   n prt phr-adj LV P Adj

◪ **5.** The gift, _____ _____ _____, **was** exquisite.

app phr-adj

n(S)   n inf phr-adj LV P Adj

⊠ **6.** The gift, _____ _____ _____, **was** exquisite.

B

- On your paper number from 1 to 8.
- Beside each number, write the appositive or appositive phrase.
- After each write the noun or pronoun it modifies (or renames) and the use of each in the sentence.
- If necessary, use the symbols to refer to the examples given on the preceding pages.

☐ **1.** During sixth period she was a student assistant a job that gave her some time for her homework.

☐ **2.** The speaker a clairvoyant of considerable renown predicted some astounding events.

⊠ **3.** Mayor Smith a person to be respected for her integrity has promised to work for lower taxes.

‖ **4.** Ida Gold a local celebrity was enthusiastically greeted.

⊟ **5.** Her brother Nelson also plays on the team.

☐ **6.** We went to her home a little bungalow on the outskirts of the town.

◪ **7.** Thoreau and Emerson both authors realizing their inheritance from Europe remained detached.

☐ **8.** Some students those who were from Niles usually expressed a different point of view.

- Number your paper again from 1 to 8.
- Beside each number write the word(s), if any, in each sentence that should be followed by commas.

SKILL TEST

- On your paper number from 1 to 8.
- Beside each number, write the appositive or appositive phrase.
- After each, write the noun or pronoun it modifies (or renames) and the use of the noun or pronoun in the sentence.

1. They are good reporters some of the best in the field.

2. The children respected their stepfather a man who had always set a good example.

3. The poem one overlooked by the literary critics for decades is exceptionally beautiful.

4. I sent the professor an authority on ancient languages the manuscript.

5. The manager a very disagreeable man was unusually unpleasant today.

6. Much symbolism can be found in *The Old Man and the Sea* Hemingway's novel that won a Pulitzer Prize in 1953.

7. She thought the woman her long lost daughter Isabelle.

8. The Vatican an interesting place to see on any tour of Rome was begun during the twelfth century.

- Number your paper again from 1 to 8.
- Beside each number write the word(s) in each sentence above that should be followed by commas.

CONCEPTS

Below is a list of labels representing the concepts that you have studied in this unit. As a review of phrases and clauses used as adjectives, look at each set of labels and try to recall the type of sentence each represents. If you have any difficulty, turn back to the appropriate page and review it before going further.

1. **a.** (S)   (_ _ _ _ _ _ _ _ _ _ _) <u>V</u> complement.
          prep phr-adj

   b. (S)   <u>LV</u>   (PN)   (_ _ _ _ _ _ _ _ _ _ _).
                  prep phr-adj

c. (S) <u>AV</u> (DO) (_ _ _ _ _ _ _ _ _ _). — prep phr-adj

d. (S) <u>AV</u> (IO) (_ _ _ _ _ _ _ _ _ _) n(DO). — prep phr-adj

e. (S) <u>AV</u> (p OP) (_ _ _ _ _ _ _ _ _ _). — prep phr-adj

2. **a.** (S) _ _ _ _ _ _ _ _ _ _ <u>V</u> complement. — prt phr-adj

b. _ _ _ _ _ _ _ _ _ _ , (S) <u>V</u> complement — prt phr-adj

c. (S) <u>LV</u> (PN) _ _ _ _ _ _ _ _ _ _ . — prt phr-adj

d. (S) <u>AV</u> (DO) _ _ _ _ _ _ _ _ _ _ . — prt phr-adj

e. (S) <u>AV</u> (IO) _ _ _ _ _ _ _ _ _ _ (DO). — prt phr-adj

f. (S) <u>AV</u> (DO) (OC) _ _ _ _ _ _ _ _ _ _ . — prt phr-adj

3. **a.** (S) _ _ _ _ _ _ _ _ _ _ <u>V</u> complement. — inf phr-adj

b. (S) <u>LV</u> (PN) _ _ _ _ _ _ _ _ _ _ . — inf phr-adj

c. (S) <u>AV</u> (DO) _ _ _ _ _ _ _ _ _ _ . — inf phr-adj

d. (S) <u>AV</u> (IO) _ _ _ _ _ _ _ _ _ _ (DO). — inf phr-adj

e. (S) <u>AV</u> (DO) (OC) _ _ _ _ _ _ _ _ _ _ . — inf phr-adj

4. **a.** (S) _ _ _ s _ _ _ _ v _ _ <u>V</u> complement. — adj cl

b. (S) <u>LV</u> (PN) _ _ _ s _ _ _ _ v _ _ . — adj cl

c. (S) <u>AV</u> (DO) _ _ _ s _ _ _ v _ _ _ . — adj cl

d. (S) <u>AV</u> (IO) _ _ s _ _ _ _ v _ _ (DO). — adj cl

                                                      adj cl

e. (S)   <u>AV</u>   (DO)   (OC)   _ _ _^s_ _ _ _ _^v_ _ .

                                                   adj cl

f. (S)   <u>AV</u>   (p   OP)   _ _ _^s_ _ _ _ _^v_ _ .

                          app-adj

5. a. (S),   _ _ _ _ⁿ_ _ _ _ ,   <u>V</u>   complement.

                               app phr-adj

b. (S),   _ _ _ _ _ _ _ _ _ _ _ _ _ _ _ _ _ _ _ⁿ_ _ _ ,   <u>V</u>   complement.

                       app phr-adj   prep phr-adj

c. (S),   _ _ _ _ _ _ _ _ _ _ _ⁿ_ _ _ _ (_ _ _ _ _ _ _), <u>V</u> complement.

                       app phr-adj   adj cl

d. (S),   _ _ _ _ _ _ _ _ _ _ _ⁿ_ _ _ _ _ _^s_ _ _ _ _^v_ _ , <u>V</u> complement.

                       app phr-adj   prt phr-adj

e. (S),   _ _ _ _ _ _ _ _ _ⁿ_ _ _ _ _ _ _ _ _ _ ,   <u>V</u>   complement.

                       app phr-adj   inf phr-adj

f. (S),   _ _ _ _ _ _ _ _ _ⁿ_ _ _ _ _ _ _ _ _ _ ,   <u>V</u>   complement.

REVIEW A

■ On a separate sheet of paper, write a sentence to fit each of the formulas listed in the Concepts section. Skip a line between each sentence.

■ Underline and label the verb or verb phrase in the main clause; label the subject and any complements.

■ Place parentheses around prepositional phrases.

■ Draw a broken line beneath all phrases and clauses used as adjectives; label and draw an arrow to the word modified.

■ Separate adjective phrases and clauses from the rest of the sentence by commas where necessary.

REVIEW B

On a separate sheet of paper, answer the following questions.

1. What is the usual location of a simple adjective (one word) in relation to the noun or pronoun it modifies?

2. What is the usual location of a prepositional phrase used as an adjective in relation to the noun or pronoun it modifies?

3. What two questions about a noun or pronoun do prepositional phrases used as adjectives answer?

4. What is the usual location of a participle used as an adjective in relation to the noun or pronoun it modifies?

5. Under what four circumstances are participial phrases separated from the rest of the sentence by commas?

6. What is a dangling participial phrase?

7. When is a participial phrase misplaced?

8. What is an infinitive? An infinitive phrase?

9. What is the location of an infinitive phrase used as an adjective in relation to the noun or pronoun it modifies?

10. What is the usual location of an adjective clause in relation to the noun or pronoun it modifies?

11. Under what four circumstances are adjective clauses separated from main clauses by commas?

12. Under what two circumstances are adjective clauses not separated from main clauses by commas?

13. What is an appositive?

14. What are the various structures that can accompany appositives in appositive phrases?

15. When is an appositive not separated from the rest of the sentence by commas?

REVIEW C

- On your paper number from 1 to 8.
- Beside each number, list each phrase and clause in the sentence that serves as an adjective.
- After each, write its kind (prepositional, participial, or infinitive phrase or adjective clause).
- Write also the noun or pronoun each modifies and the use of the noun or pronoun in the sentence.

1. Leona a young girl who has been crippled since birth has a serene disposition.

2. The last thing to add to the casserole is the buttered bread crumbs.

3. The nation's energy problem which is causing all of us much concern must be our first priority.

4. The clerk in Wards remembered the color of the dress he had sold her.

5. Tomorrow we will auction these small, used, electrical appliances donated by your company.

6. The message for Royal who had just left seemed urgent.

7. His play written in the sixteenth century has a message that is relevant today.

8. Working on the float last night the sophomores all had a very hilarious time.

■ On your paper number again from 1 to 8.
■ Beside each number write the word(s), if any, in each sentence above that should be followed by commas.

REVIEW D

■ On your paper number from 1 to 5.
■ Beside each number, list each phrase and clause in the **sentence** that serves as an adjective.
■ After each, write its kind (prepositional, participial, or infinitive phrase or adjective clause).
■ Write also the noun or pronoun each modifies and the use of the noun or pronoun in the sentence.

1. Reading in an English literature book I discovered two delightful poems written by Wordsworth.

2. The hours to register for this semester will be posted this afternoon and my chances for an early hour are very good.

3. This tiny, single-celled organism which can only be seen under a powerful microscope is the cause of the epidemic.

4. The officer gave a child whom he had never seen before the Christmas present a lovely doll dressed in a kimono.

5. Mr. Jones arriving late to work for the third consecutive day was fired instantly his boss took no time to listen to his excuses.

■ On your paper number again from 1 to 5.
■ Beside each number write the word(s), if any, in each sentence that should be followed by a mark of punctuation.
■ After each word write the appropriate mark.

GRAMMAR

STEP-BY-STEP

UNIT X

Phrases and Clauses Used as Adverbs

UNIT V

Phrases and Clauses Used as Adverbs

SKILL 1

Identifying Prepositional Phrases Used as Adverbs

Like a simple adverb (one word), a <u>prepositional phrase</u> can modify an action verb telling *how, when,* or *where* an action is performed. Study the sentences below.

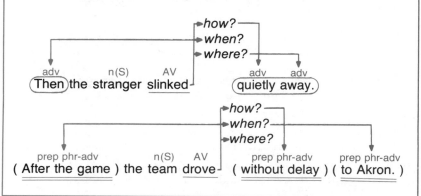

Prepositional phrases used as adverbs also respond to the question *why.* Note below.

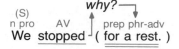

Prepositional phrases, like simple adverbs, can also modify <u>predicate adjectives</u>. Note below.

how smart?

n(S)   LV adv P Adj
His daughter <u>is</u> <u>very</u> smart.

smart how?

n(S) LV P Adj   prep phr-adv
Her son <u>is</u> smart (<u>in arithmetic.</u>)

sleepy when?

n(S) LV P Adj   prep phr-adv
The child <u>was</u> sleepy (<u>during the movie.</u>)

dark where?

(S)
n pro LV P Adj   prep phr-adv
It <u>was</u> dark (<u>in the tunnel.</u>)

A sentence can contain prepositional phrases used as adjectives and adverbs. Study the examples below.

where?
how?   *which desk?*

prep phr-adv   (S)
        n pro AV   prep phr-adv   prep phr-adj
(<u>In haste</u>) he <u>ran</u> (<u>to the desk</u>) (<u>of the night editor.</u>)

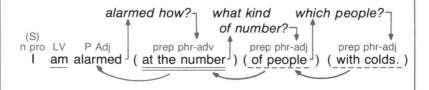

alarmed how? *what kind* *which people?*
of number?

(S)
n pro LV P Adj   prep phr-adv   prep phr-adj   prep phr-adj
I <u>am</u> alarmed (<u>at the number</u>) (<u>of people</u>) (<u>with colds.</u>)

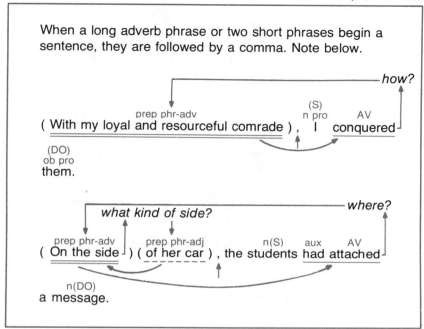

When a long adverb phrase or two short phrases begin a sentence, they are followed by a comma. Note below.

how?

prep phr-adv   (S) n pro   AV
(With my loyal and resourceful comrade) ,   I   conquered

(DO)
ob pro
them.

what kind of side?   where?

prep phr-adv   prep phr-adj   n(S)   aux   AV
(On the side) (of her car) , the students had attached

n(DO)
a message.

CHECKUP

On a separate sheet of paper answer the following questions.

1. To what four questions do prepositional phrases used as adverbs respond?
2. To what two questions do prepositional phrases used as adjectives respond?
3. Which two parts of speech do prepositional phrases used as adverbs modify?
4. Which two parts of speech do prepositional phrases used as adjectives modify?
5. When are commas placed after prepositional phrases that begin sentences?

A

■ On your paper write the sentences below.
■ Underline the verbs or verb phrases, and label the principal parts.
■ Draw a double line beneath each prepositional phrase used as an adverb; label appropriately and indicate the question to which it responds.
■ Draw an arrow to the verb or predicate adjective it modifies.

EXAMPLE:

(S)
n pro AV   prep phr-adv (where)   prep phr-adv (how)
He went (to summer school) (against his will.)

1. The customer bought this couch on credit at our suburban store during our January sale.

2. The delegate was angry about the decision; therefore, after the meeting he complained in strong language to the chairperson.

3. Against heavy and seemingly insurmountable odds, she stuck to her goals and won a gold medal in 1979 at the gymnastics tournament.

4. During that winter after her arrival, the icy wind blew across the plains toward the south with unusual and unrelenting ferocity.

5. It was rainy in the downtown area during the lunch hour, so he ran to the bank in the drizzle.

■ Explain the use of punctuation in sentences 2, 3, 4, and 5.

B

■ Number your paper from 1 to 10.
■ Beside the number, write the prepositional phrase found in the corresponding sentence.
■ After each, identify the phrase as adjective or adverb; also, write the word it modifies and the question to which it responds.

EXAMPLE:

The pies in the oven smell delicious.
(in the oven) adj pies which?

Before the test Mike studied intensely.
(Before the test) adv studied when?

1. The boy with the blonde hair hit the home run.

2. The dynamite exploded near the bridge.

3. They had built a home with six bedrooms.

4. Jack killed four mosquitoes with one blow.

5. That is a plan with many flaws.

6. Bonita is tired of her arm cast.

7. I walked his dog for a dollar.

8. My grandmother left her sons a fortune in diamonds.

9. Without a permit no one can enter.

10. The poverty of her childhood made her insecure.

C

- Number your paper from 1 to 6.
- Beside the number, write the prepositional phrases found in the corresponding sentence.
- After each, identify the phrase as adjective or adverb; also, write the word it modifies and the question to which it responds.

1. One of the boys lives across the street.

2. The laws protect children under sixteen from unjust labor practices.

3. The guide with the handlebar mustache seemed very good with the children.

4. Under the porch the dog had dug a hole about two feet deep.

5. My history professor at Purdue University was in the Normandy Invasion.

6. Jack London wrote about life in the frozen wilderness.

D

- Number your paper from 1 to 5.
- Beside the number, write the prepositional phrases found in the corresponding sentence.
- After each, identify the phrase as adjective or adverb; also, write the word it modifies and the question to which it responds.

1. For several long, difficult years the family of six lived in extreme poverty in the slums of a large eastern city.

2. After the dinner the legislators strolled with their wives into the grand ballroom for the elegant inaugural rituals.

3. During the week they stopped at the homes of several old friends from their college days for the usual chats about the past.

4. Many seemed anxious about the latest economic bulletins concerning the draught in the corn belt.

5. In spite of our warning these remained adamant in their demands for excessive increases in wages the company has been forced into bankruptcy.

■ On your paper list the numbers of those sentences that require internal punctuation.
■ Beside each number write each word in the sentence that should be followed by a mark of punctuation; after each write the appropriate mark.

SKILL TEST

■ Number your paper from 1 to 4.
■ Beside the number, write the prepositional phrases found in the corresponding sentence.
■ After each, identify the phrase as adjective or adverb; also, write the word it modifies and the question to which it responds.

1. In our community he is held in high esteem for his contribution to the arts however he never attends a cultural event.

2. During the last few days of the month her manner had become increasingly irritating to our clients.

3. Our boss addressed her complaint about the "red tape" to the president of the company and one of the managers immediately apologized to her for the inconvenience.

4. These books are a few of many he wrote for the young reader.

■ On your paper list the numbers of those sentences that require internal punctuation.
■ Beside each number write each word in the sentence that should be followed by a mark of punctuation; after each word write the appropriate mark.

REVIEW A

■ On your paper write the sentences below.
■ Underline the verb or verb phrase in each main clause, and label the principal parts.
■ Draw a broken line beneath each phrase and clause used as an adjective; label each appropriately and draw an arrow to the noun or pronoun it modifies.
■ Punctuate where necessary.

1. Their new receptionist hired last week seems very personable.

2. The player from Mexico will be a difficult person to beat this time.

3. Deserving a raise I wrote my employer a letter detailing my contributions to the business.

4. Mr. Christiansen who owns the antique store donated several interesting articles for our exhibit.

5. The scientific world thought her a genius, a woman without equal.

REVIEW B

■ On your paper write the sentences below.
■ Underline the verb or verb phrase in each main clause, and label the principal parts.
■ Place brackets above any phrase (gerund or infinitive) or clause used as a noun.
■ Label each and indicate its use in the sentence.

1. Winning in life is an all-the-time occupation.

2. The major networks made recent reports on how the economy stands at the end of this third quarter.

3. The object of the game was to tag the opponent before he or she could get back to the line.

4. The committee couldn't decide what the club should do with the remaining funds.

SKILL 2

Identifying Infinitives and Infinitive Phrases Used as Adverbs

Infinitives and infinitive phrases also function as adverbs. They usually modify the verb and respond to the usual adverb questions. Note below.

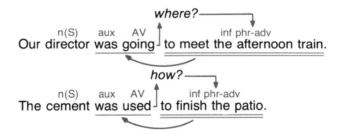

Frequently infinitive phrases used as adverbs respond to the question *why.* Note below.

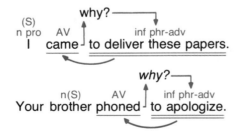

Infinitive phrases also modify <u>predicate adjectives</u>. Study the examples below.

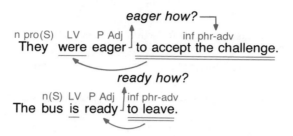

An infinitive phrase that follows a direct object often modifies it. The phrase serves as an adjective. Sometimes, however, an infinitive phrase that follows a <u>direct object</u> modifies the <u>verb</u> and serves as an <u>adverb</u>. Study the two examples below.

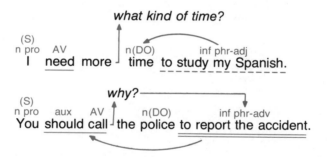

When an infinitive phrase used as an adverb begins a sentence, it is usually followed by a <u>comma</u>. Note below.

IMPORTANT

Remember that in infinitive phrases, infinitives are accompanied by complements that respond to the questions *who(m)* or *what* or modifiers that respond to the questions *how, when, where,* or *why.*

CHECKUP

Answer the following questions on a separate sheet of paper.

1. To what four questions do infinitive phrases used as adverbs respond?
2. To what two questions do infinitive phrases used as adjectives respond?
3. What two parts of speech do infinitive phrases used as adverbs modify?
4. What two parts of speech do infinitive phrases used as adjectives modify?
5. When does an infinitive phrase used as an adverb involve the use of commas?
6. What six questions does one ask to find all of the complements and modifiers that accompany an infinitive in an infinitive phrase?

A

■ On a separate sheet complete the following sentences by furnishing an appropriate infinitive phrase.

where?
        n(S)   AV   inf phr-adv
1. Mother went to _____ .

how?
        n(S)   aux aux   AV   inf phr-adv
2. The funds will be spent to _____ .

why?
        n(S)   AV   inf phr-adv
3. Mr. Ruiz called to _____ .

why?
        n(S)   AV   inf phr-adv
4. The band went (to Washington) to _____ .

how?
    (S)
    n pro   LV   P Adj   inf phr-adv
5. We were glad to _____ .

why?
                        (S)
    inf phr-adv   id pro   aux   AV   adv
6. To _____ , one must practice daily.

B

■ Number your paper from 1 to 8.
■ Beside the number, write the infinitive or infinitive phrase found in the corresponding sentence.
■ Write the word it modifies and the question to which it responds.

1. To get the best results one should take two tablets every hour.

2. The money will be used to pay for the wedding.

3. She went to call her stepfather.

4. His mumbled speech was extremely difficult to understand.

5. My secretary has written them a letter to get further information.

6. Last summer gasoline was hard to find.

7. To insure a large attendance the committee authorized free hot dogs and balloons.

8. She named the baby Sylvia to please her mother.

■ On your paper list the numbers of those sentences that require internal punctuation.
■ Beside each number write the word in each sentence that should be followed by a comma.

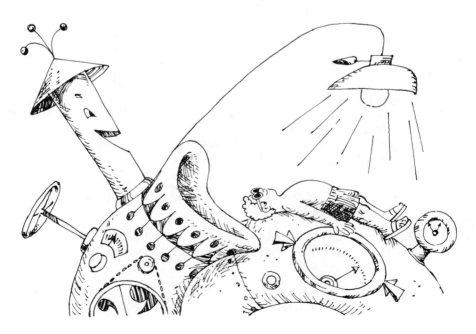

■ On your paper write each of the sentences below.
■ Underline the verb or verb phrase in each; label the principal parts.
■ Draw a double line beneath each adverb structure (prepositional or infinitive phrase); label appropriately and indicate the question each answers. Draw an arrow to the word modified.
■ Punctuate where necessary.

A. 1. We were going to the mall.

2. We are going to see a bullfight in Juarez.

B. 1. The child seemed frightened about something.

2. The child seemed frightened to be alone.

C. 1. For your success I would do anything.

2. For your sake and your family's security I would do anything.

3. To insure your success I would do anything.

D. 1. Dad put new weather stripping around the doors to save energy.

2. Alice ran to the neighbor's house to borrow a shovel.

3. After such a difficult ordeal you should go on a vacation to rest awhile.

■ Number your paper from 1 to 5.
■ Beside the number, list all phrases used as adverbs found in the corresponding sentence.
■ After each, write its kind (prepositional or infinitive), the word it modifies, and the question to which it responds.

1. You must turn this switch to start the motor then you pull this lever to the left to start the feeder.

2. In that period of time these stones were used by the women to grind peppers corn and other foods and these large jars were used to store water.

3. A ferocious dog was kept on the grounds to frighten any would-be intruders.

4. At the time several weren't psychologically prepared to go with the expedition therefore we were very hesitant to include them.

5. To protect the leather one should clean it with linseed oil.

■ Number your paper again from 1 to 5.
■ Beside each number list each word in the corresponding sentence that should be followed by a mark of punctuation.
■ After each word write the appropriate mark.

E

■ On your paper write each sentence below.
■ Underline the verb or verb phrase in each, and label the principal parts.
■ Draw a bracket above any infinitive phrase used as a noun and label appropriately.
■ Draw a broken line beneath any infinitive phrase used as an adjective; label appropriately and draw an arrow to the word modified.
■ Draw a double line beneath any infinitive phrase used as an adverb; label appropriately and indicate the question it answers; draw an arrow to the word modified.

(In each set of sentences below, there is one of each type of infinitive phrase—noun, adjective, and adverb.)

A. **1.** To ski well, one needs good coordination.

2. The office staff wants to take up a collection for his family.

3. We have found a great place to eat Chinese food.

B. **1.** My goal is to sell thirty units this week.

2. He called the editor to complain about the errors in the article.

3. This is not the time to be indecisive.

C. **1.** The best remedy to relieve sore muscles is a hot bath.

2. These are learning to write the alphabet now.

3. Some have been eager to ask you some questions.

D. **1.** He has gone to do an errand for me.

2. To buy a home now would be a wise decision.

3. Emily is shopping for a birthday gift to send her mother.

- Number your paper from 1 to 10.
- Beside the number write the infinitive or infinitive phrases found in the corresponding sentence.
- After each phrase used as a noun, write its function in the sentence **(S, PN, DO).**
- After each phrase used as an adjective, write the noun or pronoun modified and the use of the noun or pronoun in the sentence.
- After each phrase used as an adverb, write the verb or adjective it modifies and the question to which it responds.

1. Her brother had gone to catch the bus.

2. The investors are anxious to receive their dividend checks.

3. The thing to do now is to keep silent.

4. Chris would be a good person to carry out this responsibility.

5. The plumber expects to be finished by noon.

6. To build a bench around the cottonwood tree would be a fun project.

7. To complete the order, we will need you to work late.

8. My sister has given me a good example to follow.

9. To arrive in Detroit on Thursday is our present plan.

10. The former owner had paneled the wall to hide a large crack.

- Number your paper from 1 to 5.
- Beside the number, write the infinitives or infinitive phrases found in the corresponding sentence.
- After each phrase used as a noun, write its function in the sentence **(S, PN, DO).**
- After each phrase used as an adjective, write the noun or pronoun modified and the use of the noun or pronoun in the sentence.
- After each phrase used as an adverb, write the verb or adjective it modifies and the question to which it responds.

1. The magician was fascinating to watch and everyone was eager to help him with his act.

2. To make a mistake is easy but to forgive oneself is sometimes difficult.

3. Our funds to be used for the dance are meager therefore a candy drive to raise money is imperative.

4. To be a successful news commentator she first had the ability to read well moreover her attractive appearance enabled her to gain popularity quickly.

5. The refreshments decorations and favors are certain to please everyone and the floor show promises to be very entertaining.

■ Number your paper again from 1 to 5.
■ Beside each number list each word in the corresponding sentence that should be followed by a mark of punctuation.
■ After each word write the appropriate mark.

SKILL TEST

■ Number your paper from 1 to 5.
■ Beside the number, write the infinitive phrases found in the corresponding sentence.
■ After each phrase used as a noun, write its function in the sentence **(S, PN, DO).**
■ After each phrase used as an adjective, write the noun or pronoun modified and the use of the noun or pronoun in the sentence.
■ After each phrase used as an adverb, write the verb or adjective it modifies and the question to which it responds.

1. To meet their demands would be a mistake however the right to make the decision rests with you.

2. To guarantee your money's safety a police officer is placed to guard the entrance to the vault.

3. My ambition is to own a car dealership but enough money to open up my own business will be hard to earn.

4. We wanted them to buy milk doughnuts and orange juice but they purchased punch and cookies instead to serve our morning visitors.

5. Many think her chances to win in this election very good.

■ Beside each number list each word in the corresponding sentence that should be followed by a mark of punctuation.
■ After each word write the appropriate mark.

REVIEW A

■ On your paper number from 1 to 5.
■ Beside each number write the gerund phrase found in the corresponding sentence.
■ After each phrase write its function in the sentence **(S, PN, DO, OP).**

1. My little brother was punished for playing in the street.

2. Unfortunately statistics show smoking among young girls increasing.

3. His last official act will be signing this bill.

4. Everyone dislikes taking tests.

5. Swimming this river is very risky.

REVIEW B

■ On your paper write the sentences below.
■ Underline the verb or verb phrase in each main clause, and label the principal parts.
■ Draw a broken line under each phrase and clause used as an adjective; label its kind (prepositional, participial, infinitive, or appositive phrase or adjective clause). Draw an arrow to the word modified, and label the use of the noun or pronoun in the sentence.
■ Punctuate where necessary.

1. The man standing on the corner looks familiar.

2. Mrs. Emerson an outstanding commercial artist from Denver wants an opportunity to show you her portfolio.

3. The prize was a large beautiful onyx elephant from Mexico which would look great in his study.

4. Mowing the lawn every Saturday afternoon my father often saw the neighbor across the street working on her car.

5. Ms. Shimoto who became discouraged by the high bidding left the auction.

SKILL 3

Identifying and Punctuating Sentences Containing Adverb Clauses

Subordinate clauses can serve not only as nouns and adjectives but also as adverbs. Study the examples below.

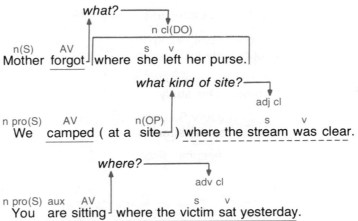

what?

n cl(DO)

n(S)   AV   s   v
Mother forgot ⌐ where she left her purse.

what kind of site?

adj cl

n pro(S)   AV   n(OP)   s   v
We   camped (at a site ⌐) where the stream was clear.

where?

adv cl

n pro(S) aux   AV   s   v
You   are sitting ⌐ where the victim sat yesterday.

Use the letters *adv cl* to indicate an *adverb clause.*

Adverb clauses respond to the usual adverb questions *how, when, where,* and *why.* Note below.

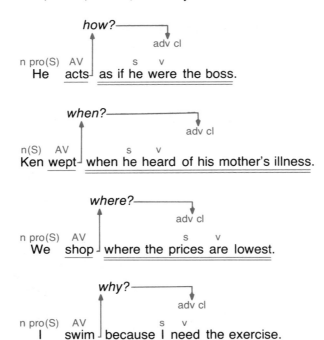

how?

adv cl

n pro(S)   AV   s   v
He   acts┘ as if he were the boss.

when?

adv cl

n(S)   AV   s   v
Ken wept┘ when he heard of his mother's illness.

where?

adv cl

n pro(S)   AV   s   v
We   shop┘ where the prices are lowest.

why?

adv cl

n pro(S)   AV   s   v
I   swim┘ because I need the exercise.

Some subordinate clauses that follow direct objects modify them and are adjective clauses. Other subordinate clauses that follow direct objects modify the verb and are <u>adverb clauses</u>.

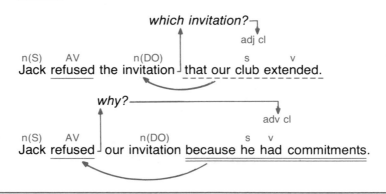

which invitation?

adj cl

n(S)   AV   n(DO)   s   v
Jack refused the invitation┘ that our club extended.

why?

adv cl

n(S)   AV   n(DO)   s   v
Jack refused┘ our invitation because he had commitments.

Adverb clauses can modify <u>predicate adjectives</u>. Study the examples below.

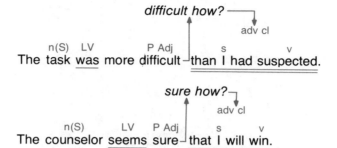

Like simple adverbs, adverb clauses can usually be moved around in a sentence. Study the examples below.

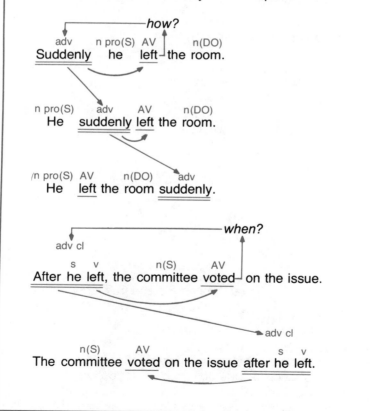

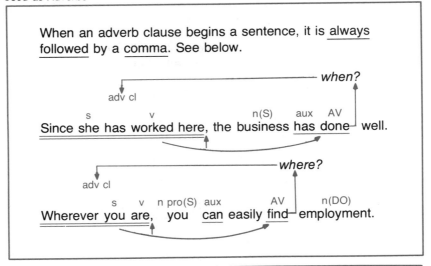

When an adverb clause begins a sentence, it is <u>always</u> <u>followed</u> by a <u>comma</u>. See below.

Words that usually begin adverb clauses are the following:

after	than
although	though
as	unless
as if	until
because	when
before	whenever
if	where
since	wherever
so that	while

CHECKUP

Answer the following questions on a separate sheet of paper.

1. What is a clause?
2. What is a subordinate clause?
3. What is a main clause?
4. What are the three kinds of subordinate clauses?
5. To what questions do adverb clauses respond?
6. What two parts of speech do adverb clauses modify?
7. When does an adverb clause require the use of a comma?

A

■ On a separate sheet complete the following sentences by furnishing an appropriate adverb clause.

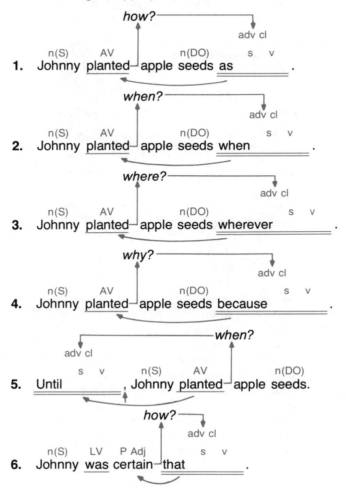

1. Johnny planted apple seeds as _____ .

2. Johnny planted apple seeds when _____ .

3. Johnny planted apple seeds wherever _____ .

4. Johnny planted apple seeds because _____ .

5. Until _____ , Johnny planted apple seeds.

6. Johnny was certain that _____ .

B

■ Number your paper from 1 to 10.
■ Beside each number, write the adverb clause found in the corresponding sentence, and indicate its subject and verb.
■ Write the word it modifies and the question to which it responds.

1. Nero fiddled while Rome burned.

2. They own a cabin where the Green River divides.

3. An accused woman was guilty unless she could prove herself innocent.

4. If the dam breaks the entire city will flood.

5. The school will not award you a diploma unless you have earned enough credits.

6. We left the meeting early because a storm was approaching.

7. Dad is positive that he can be there tomorrow.

8. As the parade passed the stands the mayor's wife applauded.

9. She played the entire game although she has a broken rib.

10. Since I quit my job in the afternoon my grades have improved.

■ On your paper list the numbers of those sentences that require internal punctuation.
■ Beside each number write the word in each sentence that should be followed by a comma.

■ On your paper write each sentence below.
■ Underline the verb or verb phrase in each main clause, and label the principal parts.
■ Draw a bracket above any subordinate clause used as a noun; indicate its subject and verb; identify its function in the sentence.
■ Draw a broken line beneath any subordinate clause used as an adjective; indicate its subject and verb, label appropriately, and draw an arrow to the noun or pronoun it modifies.
■ Draw a double line beneath any subordinate clause used as an adverb; label appropriately, indicate its subject and verb, and draw an arrow to the word it modifies.

A. 1. The sketch that I made of the administration building is still hanging in the art room.

2. I did the sketch when I was a sophomore here.

3. Why it has remained there is a mystery to me.

B. 1. My family visited Washington, D.C., which has an abundance of tourist attractions.

2. While we were there, we found the humidity insufferable.

3. The Smithsonian Institute was what we enjoyed most.

C. **1.** Chris was feeling ill as he walked to school this morning.

2. He said that his head and joints were aching.

3. I will take Chris his books, which he left in the nurse's office.

D

■ On your paper write each sentence below.

■ Underline the verb or verb phrase in each; label the principal parts.

■ Draw a double line beneath each adverb structure (prepositional or infinitive phrase or adverb clause); label appropriately and indicate the question each answers. Draw an arrow to the word modified.

■ Punctuate where necessary.

A. **1.** Your car will be ready in the morning.

2. Your car will be expensive to fix properly.

3. Your car will be unattractive until it can be repainted.

B. **1.** Before breakfast Sonia left for the airport.

2. Before I could get breakfast she left for the airport.

3. To secure her place on the flight she left for the airport early.

C. **1.** She usually plays tennis in the afternoon.

2. To stay in shape she plays tennis in the afternoon.

3. To stay in shape she plays tennis in the afternoon after she finishes her classes.

D. **1.** During the last student council meeting the students wrote the editor to complain about the school traffic problem.

2. Because accidents were occurring too frequently the students wrote the editor a letter to complain about the school traffic problem.

CONCEPTS

Below is a list of labels representing the concepts that you have studied in this unit. As a review of phrases and clauses used as adverbs, look at each set of labels and try to recall the type of sentence each represents. If you have any difficulty, turn back to the appropriate section and review it before going further.

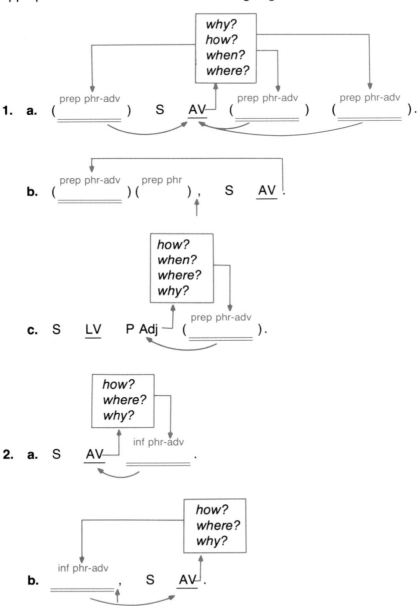

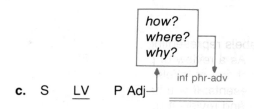

c. S LV P Adj⌐ inf phr-adv

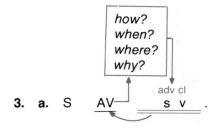

3. a. S AV⌐ adv cl s v .

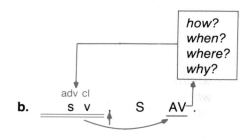

b. adv cl s v S AV .

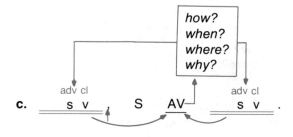

c. adv cl s v S AV⌐ adv cl s v .

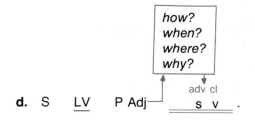

d. S LV P Adj⌐ adv cl s v .

REVIEW A

■ On a sheet of paper, write a sentence to fit each of the formulas listed in the Concepts section. Skip a line between each sentence.

■ Underline the verb or verb phrase in each main clause; label the subject and any complements.

■ Draw a double line beneath any adverb structure (phrase or clause). Label and indicate the question each answers. Draw an arrow to the word modified.

■ Indicate the subject and verb in each subordinate clause.

■ Punctuate where necessary.

REVIEW B

■ On a separate sheet of paper, answer the following questions.

1. To which four questions do adverb phrases and clauses respond?

2. Which two parts of speech do adverb phrases and clauses usually modify?

3. Other than the simple adverb (one word), what are the three types of adverb structures?

4. When do phrases and clauses used as adverbs involve commas?

REVIEW C

■ Number your paper from 1 to 5.

■ Beside each number, list all phrases and clauses used as adverbs found in the corresponding sentence.

■ Write its kind (prepositional or infinitive phrase or adverb clause), the word it modifies, and the question to which it responds.

■ Beside each number list each word, if any, in the corresponding sentence that should be followed by a comma.

1. Because he is a reputable person our judgment should be delayed until all facts have been studied.

2. To meet the deadline the papers should be mailed to her as soon as the printer delivers them to us.

3. When we were getting the house ready for sale we repainted the living room to match the carpeting.

4. During the noisy tribal dances the scout crept into the captives' tents to explain the plan for their escape.

5. The damage is impossible to estimate accurately.

GRAMMAR

STEP-BY-STEP

UNIT VI

Correct

Verb Usage

UNIT VI

Correct Verb Usage

SKILL 1

Making Verbs and Simple Subjects Agree in Number

A verb that ends in *s* is always <u>singular</u> and should only be used with a singular subject, a subject representing a unit of one. Note below.

Singular Subjects   **Singular Verbs**

(Nouns and pronouns
representing units
of one.)

He	trie(s).
Each	seem(s).
This	work(s).
Gloria	prefer(s).
The hen	cluck(s).
The engine	smell(s).

Because verbs ending in *s* are singular, they can be used with all singular noun subjects. In the examples below the number 1 represents singular.

1   1
The horse <u>neighs</u>.
1   1
The engine <u>whistles</u>.
1   1
The student <u>studies</u>.

Singular verbs
end in *s*.

Because verbs ending in *s* are singular, they can <u>never</u> be used with plural noun subjects. In the examples below the number 2 represents plural.

2   1
Horses <u>neighs</u>.

2   1
Engines <u>whistles</u>.

2   1
Students <u>studies</u>.

Singular verbs end in *s*.

A verb <u>not</u> ending in *s* is <u>plural</u> and must be used with plural noun subjects. See below.

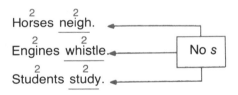

2   2
Horses <u>neigh</u>.

2   2
Engines <u>whistle</u>.

2   2
Students <u>study</u>.

No *s*

The singular verb (ending in *s*) is also used with <u>singular nominative pronouns</u>; however, there are two important exceptions. Note below.

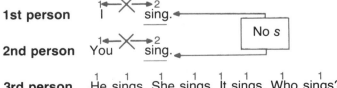

1st person   I   sing.

2nd person   You   sing.

No *s*

3rd person   He <u>sings</u>. She <u>sings</u>. It <u>sings</u>. Who <u>sings</u>?

Plural verbs (not ending in *s*) are used with <u>plural nominative pronouns</u> (we, you, and they).

Singular verbs (ending in *s*) are also used with <u>indefinite pronouns</u> that are singular. Note the singular pronouns circled below.

any*	(anyone)	(anybody)	(anything)
(each)	(everyone)	(everybody)	(everything)
none*	(no one)	(nobody)	(nothing)
some*	(someone)	(somebody)	(something)

few	(one)
several	(other)
many	(another)
more*	(either)
most*	(neither)
all*	both

Everyone loves.

Nothing vanishes.

Somebody remembers.

*Asterisks indicate pronouns that can be both singular and plural.

Remember singular verbs end in s.

IMPORTANT

Although the pronouns <u>everyone</u> and <u>everybody</u> seem to be plural, they are singular. Each represents a unit of one; each is used with the singular verb (ending in *s*).

The indefinite pronouns listed that are followed by asterisks can be both singular and plural. They are singular when they refer to singular nouns. Study the examples below.

(Cheese)   None was moldy.

(Paint)   None is dry.

They are plural when they refer to plural nouns. See below.

(Students)   None leave at noon.

(Bottles)   None break easily.

Only four indefinite pronouns are plural. They are never used with singular verbs.

Few attend.   Many enjoy.

Several disagree.   Both dance.

Two demonstrative pronouns are singular and are used as subjects to singular verbs. Two are plural and are used as subjects to plural verbs. Note below.

That fits.   These arrive.

This fits.   Those arrive.

When a singular subject is used with a singular verb (child paints) or a plural subject is used with a plural verb (children paint), the subject and verb are said to agree in number.

When a sentence contains a verb phrase, the first auxiliary verb must agree with the subject in number.

       1   1
    n(S) aux   AV
The glass is broken.

       2   2
    n(S) aux   AV
The glasses are broken.

        1   1
    n(S)   aux aux   AV
The package has been mailed.

        2   2
    n(S)   aux aux   AV
The packages have been mailed.

When the verb precedes the subject (inverted sentence), care must be taken to insure that the subject and verb agree in number. Study the examples below.

       1   1
P Adv LV   n(S)
Here is the book.

      1   1
    LV   n(S)
Here' s the book.   (Singular verb can be contracted.)

       2   2
P Adv LV   n(S)
Here are the books.

      1 ✕ 2
    LV   n(S)   Wrong
Here' s the books. (Plural verb cannot be contracted.)

In a question, care must also be taken to insure that the subject and verb agree in number. Study the examples.

    1   1
aux   n(S)   AV
Has the teacher left?

   2   2
LV n pro(S)   P Adj
Are they dependable?

A verb must agree in number with the subject and never with a noun or pronoun in a prepositional phrase. Note below.

One (of them) studies here.

CHECKUP

Answer the following questions on a separate sheet of paper.

1. How can a singular verb be identified?
2. How can a plural verb be identified?
3. What are the singular nominative pronouns? Which two are used with plural verbs?
4. Which indefinite pronouns are singular? Which are plural? Which can be both singular and plural?
5. What is meant when subjects and verbs are said to agree in number?

A

■ If the word **one** sounds correct before a noun, the noun is singular. If the word **two** sounds right placed before a noun, the noun is plural. Test the nouns below by mentally placing the word **one** or **two** before them.

■ On a separate sheet of paper, beside the corresponding number, identify whether the noun is singular or plural.

1. sheriff	10. mouse	19. wolves	28. herd
2. trips	11. children	20. team	29. system
3. men	12. city	21. pair	30. teeth
4. troop	13. gang	22. feet	31. knives
5. fleet	14. cupful	23. tomatoes	32. collection
6. halves	15. valleys	24. class	33. pastries
7. fox	16. price	25. leaves	34. women
8. radio	17. roof	26. enemies	35. quarts
9. gases	18. calves	27. goose	36. group

B

■ Study the information about indefinite pronouns on page 205.
■ Then without referring to these pages, list on a separate sheet in separate columns those indefinite pronouns that are plural, those that are singular, and those that can be either singular or plural.

C

■ On a separate sheet beside the corresponding numbers, write the nouns and pronouns below.
■ Place a number **1** above those that are singular, a **2** above those that are plural.
■ Write a singular verb (ending in *s*) after each singular noun or pronoun.

1. each	11. he	21. parent	31. those
2. this	12. several	22. flock	32. area
3. stories	13. crowd	23. neither	33. anyone
4. either	14. someone	24. these	34. many
5. teachers	15. children	25. college	35. it
6. we	16. lens	26. few	36. mice
7. vacation	17. that	27. nobody	37. both
8. everyone	18. people	28. geese	38. woman
9. ladies	19. no one	29. everybody	39. they
10. somebody	20. all	30. oxen	40. she

D

■ On a separate sheet beside the corresponding number, write the verbs and verb phrases below.
■ Place a **1** above each singular verb or verb phrase.
■ Place a **2** above each plural verb or verb phrase.

1. quit	6. appears	11. speak	16. were saved
2. tell	7. has hit	12. does become	17. have complained
3. is	8. is decided	13. seems	18. finishes
4. like	9. knows	14. grow	19. was brought
5. taste	10. enjoys	15. are	20. are going

- ■ On a separate sheet, write the sentences below.
- ■ Underline the verb or verb phrase in each.
- ■ Write a **1** above each subject and each verb that is singular.
- ■ Write a **2** above each subject and each verb that is plural.
- ■ Place a **C** before each sentence if the subject and verb agree. Correct the verbs in the other sentences.

1. The girl thinks well.

2. This seems fair.

3. Both sees clearly.

4. He don't know.

5. That doesn't work.

6. Several take lessons.

7. They goes daily.

8. Neither are sure.

9. Everybody has left.

10. One have reported.

11. We were deceived.

12. It don't fit.

- ■ On a separate sheet, rewrite the sentences below by placing the subject before the verb.
- ■ Label the subject and verb or verb phrase in each.

EXAMPLE: Here's the file.   The file is here.

Has the secretary left?   The secretary has left.

1. Is the child ready?

2. Are both coming?

3. Then comes the dessert.

4. Does a copy remain here?

5. There's the letter carrier.

6. Weren't the packages wrapped?

7. Here's the best one.

8. Have the doctors arrived?

9. Is the soup hot?

10. Down the street came the clowns.

G

■ On a separate sheet, write the sentences below.
■ Underline the verb or verb phrase in each.
■ Write a **1** above each subject and each verb that is singular.
■ Write a **2** above each subject and each verb that is plural.
■ Place a **C** before each sentence if the subject and verb agree.
  Correct the verbs in the other sentences.

1. Where is the letter?
2. Now is the proper time.
3. Here's the paint brushes.
4. There are the onions.
5. Where's those keys?
6. Here's my idea.
7. Here is the telephone numbers.
8. There are several good hotels.
9. Where's the tickets?
10. There is a superb movie nearby.
11. Where are the announcements?
12. Then comes the difficult tasks.

H

■ On a separate sheet, write the sentences below.
■ Underline the verb or verb phrase in each.
■ Write a **1** above each subject and each verb that is singular.
■ Write a **2** above each subject and each verb that is plural.
■ Place a **C** before each sentence if the subject and verb agree.
  Correct the verbs in the other sentences.

If the group was *congenial*, it was sociable and pleasant.

1. Has the student been given a pass?
2. Was the grades posted today?
3. Were the group congenial?
4. Is anyone home?
5. Do some secretaries attend?
6. Has both moved away?
7. Wasn't those late?
8. Has the package arrived?
9. Were the letters mailed?
10. Don't he understand?
11. Have the gang been notified?
12. Are the crowd big?

I

■ On a separate sheet beside the corresponding number, write the subject of each sentence below.

■ Indicate whether the subject is singular or plural by writing **1** or **2** above it.

■ After each subject write the verb that agrees with it in number; write a **1** or **2** above it indicating singular or plural.

1. Some members of the club (**was** / **were**) disappointed in the dance.

2. A group of reporters (**was** / **were**) talking outside.

3. Where (**is** / **are**) the records of the graduating seniors?

4. Neither of the volumes (**is** / **are**) on the shelf.

5. A set of dishes (**was** / **were**) the prize.

6. A guest from one of the northern states (**refuses** / **refuse**) to eat okra.

7. The effects of the hurricane (**doesn't** / **don't**) seem too severe.

8. Everything in the boxes (**has** / **have**) been broken.

9. (**Aren't** / **Isn't**) the team ready?

10. All of the sheep (**is** / **are**) in the south pasture.

11. (**Here's** / **Here are**) your negatives from the studio.

12. (**Doesn't** / **Don't**) she like the dress?

J

■ On a separate sheet beside the corresponding number, write the subject of each sentence below.

■ Indicate whether the subject is singular or plural by writing **1** or **2** above it.

■ After each subject write the verb that agrees with it in number; write a **1** or **2** above it indicating singular or plural.

1. A player on one of the other teams (**has** / **have**) won the award.

2. (**There's** / **There are**) the storage boxes.

3. None of the punch (**was** / **were**) spilled.

4. None of the pencils (**has** / **have**) been missing.

5. (**Doesn't** / **Don't**) everybody listen to the news?

6. Either of the suitcases (**is** / **are**) large enough.

7. (**Where's** / **Where are**) the last print-outs?

8. Many fragments of the space ship (**has** / **have**) been recovered.

9. (**Does** / **Do**) everyone in the math classes participate?

10. Each of the players (**says** / **say**) a few words.

11. (**Hasn't** / **Haven't**) the flowers in this arrangement faded?

12. Now (**comes** / **come**) the difficult decisions.

SKILL TEST

■ On a separate sheet beside the corresponding number, write the subject of each sentence below.

■ Indicate whether the subject is singular or plural by writing **1** or **2** above it.

■ After each subject write the verb that agrees with it in number; write a **1** or **2** above it indicating singular or plural.

1. (**Here's** / **Here are**) some recent articles on the subject.

2. Neither (**is** / **are**) perfect in shape.

3. An investigator from one of the government agencies (**was** / **were**) here.

4. (**Is** / **Are**) everybody happy about the change?

5. Several samples of material (**was** / **were**) shown on the chart.

6. It (**doesn't** / **don't**) affect the price.

7. (**Was** / **Were**) the class dismissed early?

8. Then (**comes** / **come**) the final touches.

9. A few of the group (**speaks** / **speak**) Spanish fluently.

10. (**Where's** / **Where are**) the clients' addresses?

SKILL 2

Making Verbs and Compound Subjects Agree in Number

Compound subjects joined by the conjunctions *and* and *both . . . and* are usually plural in number and are used with plural verbs. Study the examples below.

$$
\begin{array}{cccccc}
1 & & 1 & 2 & \\
n(S) & cj & n(S) & LV & n(PN)
\end{array}
$$

Darryl (and) Jennifer <u>are</u> finalists.

$$
\begin{array}{cccccc}
2 & & 2 & & 2 & \\
cj & n(S) & cj & n(S) & aux & AV
\end{array}
$$

(Both) actors (and) musicians <u>were invited</u>.

A compound subject joined by *and* can be singular when both subjects refer to a single person or thing. In such cases the singular verb form is used. Study the examples below.

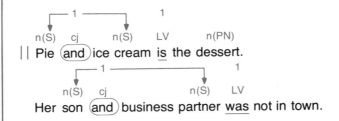

Pie (and) ice cream <u>is</u> the dessert.

Her son (and) business partner <u>was</u> not in town.

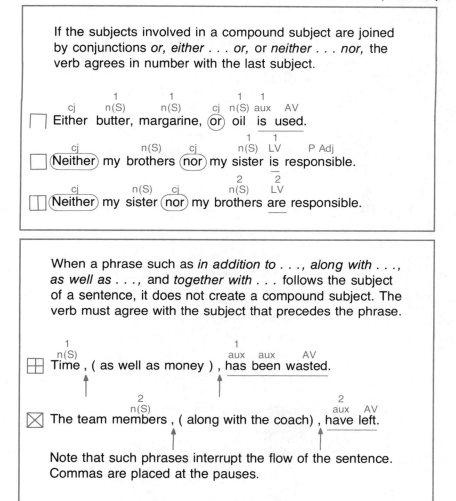

If the subjects involved in a compound subject are joined by conjunctions *or, either . . . or,* or *neither . . . nor,* the verb agrees in number with the last subject.

Either butter, margarine, (or) oil is used.

(Neither) my brothers (nor) my sister is responsible.

(Neither) my sister (nor) my brothers are responsible.

When a phrase such as *in addition to . . ., along with . . ., as well as . . .,* and *together with . . .* follows the subject of a sentence, it does not create a compound subject. The verb must agree with the subject that precedes the phrase.

Time , (as well as money) , has been wasted.

The team members , (along with the coach) , have left.

Note that such phrases interrupt the flow of the sentence. Commas are placed at the pauses.

CHECKUP

Answer the following questions on a separate sheet of paper.

1. What kind of verb usually agrees with a compound subject joined by *and?*
2. When does a compound subject joined by *and* take a singular verb form?
3. If the conjunctions *or, either . . . or,* or *neither . . . nor* join singular subjects, what form of verb is necessary?
4. If the subjects of a compound subject are both singular and plural and the conjunctions are *or, either . . . or,* or *neither . . . nor,* when is the singular verb used? When is the plural verb used?

A

■ On a separate sheet beside the corresponding number, write the subject or subjects in each sentence below and any conjunctions that connect them.

■ Indicate whether each subject is singular or plural by writing a **1** or **2** above it.

■ Note carefully the conjunctions used; then after the subject(s), choose the verb that agrees in number. Write a **1** or **2** above it.

■ If necessary, use the symbols to refer back to the examples presented earlier.

1. The book and cap (**was** / **were**) left here.

2. Macaroni and cheese (**is** / **are**) served on Monday.

3. Neither Connie, Debbie, nor Stacy (**is** / **are**) eligible.

4. The coaches or he (**makes** / **make**) the decision.

5. The teacher or his student aides (**checks** / **check**) the book numbers.

6. This donation, in addition to yours, (**brings** / **bring**) us to our goal.

7. The chorus members, together with the band, (**fills** / **fill**) the first six rows.

B

- On a separate sheet beside the corresponding number, write the subject or subjects in each sentence below and any conjunctions that connect them.
- Indicate whether each subject is singular or plural by writing a **1** or **2** above it.
- Note carefully the conjunctions used; then after the subject(s), choose the verb that agrees in number. Write a **1** or **2** above it.
- If necessary, use the symbols to refer back to the examples presented earlier.

1. His daughter and only heir (**has** / **have**) been injured seriously.

2. Either the counselor or his friends (**gives** / **give**) him extra help.

3. The girls, as well as their sponsor, (**contributes** / **contribute**) much to our school spirit.

4. Both the student and teacher (**makes** / **make**) an effort.

5. His investors or his banker (**provides** / **provide**) the extra cash.

6. A knife, dagger, or other sharp instrument (**was** / **were**) used.

7. Veronica, along with her sister, (**competes** / **compete**) in gymnastics.

C

- On a separate sheet beside the corresponding number, write the subject or subjects in each sentence below and any conjunctions that connect them.
- Indicate whether each subject is singular or plural by writing a **1** or **2** above it.
- After the subject(s), choose the verb that agrees in number; write a **1** or **2** above it.
- Check carefully to see if the subject(s) and verb agree.

1. The textbooks and workbooks (**is** / **are**) stored in the library.

2. Neither my brother nor his friends (**likes** / **like**) the location for the prom.

3. The President, along with his cabinet, (**thinks** / **think**) the measure inflationary.

4. Strawberries and cream (**is** / **are**) the dessert for the luncheon.

5.   Mayonnaise or salad dressing (**works** / **work**) equally well.

6.   Both the charcoal and the matches for the cook-out
     (**was** / **were**) left at home.

7.   My mother and I (**is** / **are**) addressing envelopes.

8.   Either the officers or their captain (**was** / **were**) negligent.

9.   Either Barbara, Sherri, or Donna (**has** / **have**) been given this
     assignment.

10. There (**was** / **were**) only a store and a service station in the
     town.

- On a separate sheet beside the corresponding number, write the
  subject or subjects in each sentence below and any conjunctions
  that connect them.
- Indicate whether each subject is singular or plural by writing a **1**
  or **2** above it.
- After the subject(s), choose the verb that agrees in number; write
  a **1** or **2** above it.
- Check carefully to see if the subject(s) and verb agree.

1.   His mother and grandmother (**keeps** / **keep**) her childhood
     artwork.

2.   Ham and eggs (**was** / **were**) his choice for breakfast.

3.   This loan, in addition to the others, (**has** / **have**) put you in a
     tight financial situation.

4.   Either he or the snake (**leaves** / **leave**).

5.   Each of them frequently (**sends** / **send**) the company letters of
     complaint.

6.   (**Is** / **Are**) many still working?

7.   Both firefighters and police officers in our community
     (**has** / **have**) decided to strike.

8.   Either the players or the coach (**needs** / **need**) a change of
     scene.

9.   (**Here is** / **Here are**) the test results.

10. Neither their sponsor nor the students (**considers** / **consider**)
     the idea a good one.

SKILL TEST

■ Beside the corresponding number, write the subject or subjects in each sentence below and any conjunctions that connect them.

■ Indicate whether each subject is singular or plural by writing a **1** or **2** above it.

■ After the subject(s), choose the verb that agrees in number; write a **1** or **2** above it.

■ Check carefully to see if the subject(s) and verb agree.

1. Neither sugar nor white flour (**is** / **are**) on my diet.

2. (**Here's** / **Here are**) the new typewriter ribbon.

3. Either she or we (**takes** / **take**) tickets at the west gate.

4. (**Is** / **Are**) the crowds big at Disneyland in January?

5. Many like me (**thinks** / **think**) him guilty.

6. (**Where's** / **Where are**) the sheets for my bed?

7. Both the parents and the daughter (**has** / **have**) complained about the regulation.

8. Calvin, as well as Norma, (**does** / **do**) this service every day for our handicapped students.

REVIEW A

■ On a separate sheet, write the sentences below.

■ Place a bracket above each verbal phrase or clause used as a noun; label its use in the sentence. Label all other words.

1. Whatever happens is your fault.

2. I find jumping rope a very good exercise.

3. Mom wants me to clean my room now.

4. Acting your very best will get you the coveted award.

5. I must decide what is best for me.

6. Peace can only be maintained by communicating freely.

7. The country considers what you did highly commendable.

8. To quit now would be disastrous.

9. The next step is to add the lemon juice.

10. The pamphlet reminded us of what we should do in an emergency.

SKILL 3

Using Correct Verb Forms

Verbs change in form to indicate time (or tense). Their three main forms are referred to as <u>present</u>, <u>past</u>, and <u>past participle</u>. Study the chart below.

Present	**Past**	**Past Participle**
Now I do	Yesterday I <u>did</u>	In the past I <u>have done</u>
Now I <u>sing</u>	Yesterday I <u>sang</u>	In the past I <u>have sung</u>
Now I <u>see</u>	Yesterday I <u>saw</u>	In the past I <u>have seen</u>

Note above that the past tense verbs are used alone. They should never be preceded by auxiliary verbs. Study the examples below.

✔I <u>did</u> not I <u>have did</u> ✕
✔I <u>sang</u> not I <u>have sang</u> ✕
✔I <u>saw</u> not I <u>have saw</u> ✕

Note also that the past participle forms are <u>always</u> used in verb phrases. They are incorrectly used when used alone as the verb of the sentence. Study the examples below.

✔I <u>have done</u> not I <u>done</u> ✕
✔I <u>have sung</u> not I <u>sung</u> ✕
✔I <u>have seen</u> not I <u>seen</u> ✕

Study the list that follows. Using the pronoun *I* as the subject of each verb, read the list orally several times to train the ear to the sound of the past tense form without the auxiliary verb and the past participle with the auxiliary verb.

CHART 1

Present	Past	Past Participle
become	became	have* become
begin	began	have begun
blow	blew	have blown
break	broke	have broken
choose	chose	have chosen
come	came	have come
do	did	have done
drink	drank	have drunk
eat	ate	have eaten
fall	fell	have fallen
fly	flew	have flown
freeze	froze	have frozen
give	gave	have given
go	went	have gone
grow	grew	have grown
know	knew	have known
ride	rode	have ridden
ring	rang	have rung
run	ran	have run
see	saw	have seen
shrink	shrank	have shrunk
speak	spoke	have spoken
steal	stole	have stolen
swim	swam	have swum
take	took	have taken
throw	threw	have thrown
wear	wore	have worn
write	wrote	have written

*Other auxiliary verbs such as has, had, is, are, was, were, has been, should have also precede the past participle form.

The past and past participle forms of many verbs are spelled identically; a single form is used with and without the auxiliary verb. This group of verbs, unlike the previous group, presents no special problem. Study the chart below.

CHART 2

Present	Past	Past Participle
bend	bent	have bent
bring	brought	have brought
burst	burst	have burst
catch	caught	have caught
dig	dug	have dug
drag	dragged*	have dragged*
drown	drowned*	have drowned*
finish	finished*	have finished*
improve	improved*	have improved*
learn	learned*	have learned*
open	opened*	have opened*
promise	promised*	have promised*
slice	sliced*	have sliced*
turn	turned*	have turned*
type	typed*	have typed*
wait	waited*	have waited*
wish	wished*	have wished*

*Note that both the past tense and past participle forms of many verbs are formed by adding *ed.*

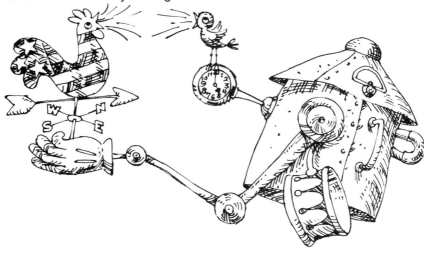

CHECKUP

Answer the following questions on a separate sheet of paper.

1. What are the three main forms of a verb called?
2. Which verb tense must never be used with an auxiliary verb?
3. Which verb tense must always be used with an auxiliary verb?

A

- Study carefully the present, past, and past participle forms of the verbs listed in Chart 1.
- Then have another person "call out" the present tense form of each verb using the pronoun *I* as the subject of each. After each present tense verb, you give the past and past participle forms.
- Make a list of the verb forms that you cannot remember correctly.
- Study your list carefully and repeat the above procedures until you can state all verbs correctly.

B

- Study carefully the present, past, and past participle forms of the verbs listed in Chart 2.
- Pay particular attention to the forms of the verbs *bring, burst, drag,* and *drown.*
- Write the three forms of these four verbs.

C

- Without referring to the previous pages, write on a separate sheet under columns labeled <u>present</u>, <u>past</u>, and <u>past participle</u> the forms of the following verbs.

1.	become	9.	fall	17.	ring	25.	throw
2.	begin	10.	fly	18.	run	26.	wear
3.	broke	11.	freeze	19.	see	27.	write
4.	choose	12.	give	20.	shrink	28.	bend
5.	come	13.	go	21.	speak	29.	bring
6.	do	14.	grow	22.	steal	30.	burst
7.	drink	15.	know	23.	swim	31.	drag
8.	eat	16.	ride	24.	take	32.	drown

■ Write the sentences below using the correct verb.
■ Underline and label the verb or verb phrase.
■ Place parentheses around prepositional phrases.
■ Label the principal parts in each sentence.

1. We could have (**went** / **gone**) with them.
2. Albert (**run** / **ran**) to the neighbors for help.
3. The voters have (**chose** / **chosen**) her their new mayor.
4. Several (**become** / **became**) his supporters in the last election.
5. Many have (**wrote** / **written**) us letters of protest.
6. They had (**ate** / **eaten**) on the plane.
7. I (**wore** / **worn**) this suit to the dance last night.
8. She (**sung** / **sang**) my favorite song.
9. I (**seen** / **saw**) the entire incident.
10. Everyone had (**grew** / **grown**) weary of the task.

■ Write the sentences below using the correct verb.
■ Underline and label the verb or verb phrase.
■ Place parentheses around prepositional phrases.
■ Label the principal parts in each sentence.

1. Last week he (**seen** / **saw**) her in the shopping mall.
2. The child had (**fell** / **fallen**) from the tree.
3. Ms. Tai (**drunk** / **drank**) a glass of warm milk at bedtime.
4. The mail (**come** / **came**) around noon.
5. The pond has (**froze** / **frozen**) early this year.
6. The students have (**began** / **begun**) the last unit.
7. The sweatshirt (**shrunk** / **shrank**) about two sizes.
8. Had she (**rode** / **ridden**) on a horse before?
9. After his illness the debts (**became** / **become**) a serious worry to him.
10. I (**did** / **done**) her several favors.

■ On a separate sheet of paper, write sentences to follow the directions given below.

1. Write a sentence using the past tense form of the verb <u>drag</u>.

2. Write a sentence using the past tense form of the verb <u>ring</u>.

3. Write a sentence using the past tense form of the verb <u>throw</u>.

4. Write a sentence using the past tense form of the verb <u>become</u>.

5. Write a sentence using the present tense form of the verb <u>drive</u>.

6. Write a sentence using the past participle form of the verb <u>burst</u>.

7. Write a sentence using the past participle form of the verb <u>bring</u>.

8. Write a sentence using the past participle form of the verb <u>swim</u>.

9. Write a sentence using the past participle form of the verb <u>know</u>.

10. Write a sentence using the past participle form of the verb <u>take</u>.

11. Write a sentence using the past tense form of the verb <u>catch</u>.

12. Write a sentence using the past participle form of the verb <u>catch</u>.

13. Write a sentence using the past tense form of the verb <u>learn</u>.

14. Write a sentence using the past participle form of the verb <u>learn</u>.

G

■ On a separate sheet beside the corresponding number, write the correct verb for each sentence below.

1. Vernon (**knew** / **knowed**) his license number.

2. Several of the crew were (**drownded** / **drowned**) during the storm.

3. We (**dragged** / **drug**) the heavy boxes to the loading dock of the old warehouse.

4. The baby (**growed** / **grew**) very tired and restless during the long meeting.

5. Then the bubbles quickly (**burst** / **bursted**).

6. My sister (**catched** / **caught**) the biggest northern pike measured during the season.

7. The wind (**blew** / **blowed**) the fallen leaves against the freshly painted fence.

8. He (**throwed** / **threw**) three consecutive strikes to the league's best hitter.

9. Some of the spectators had (**brung** / **brought**) umbrellas.

10. The pirates (**digged** / **dug**) for the treasure.

11. She (**swam** / **swimmed**) the English Channel last summer.

12. The twins (**brang** / **brought**) the refreshments.

■ Number your paper from 1 to 12.
■ If a sentence has no errors in verb forms, write **C** after the corresponding number.
■ If a sentence contains an incorrect verb form, rewrite the sentence correcting the error.

1. Yesterday she drived to Madison.

2. The steaks for tonight are still frozen.

3. I seen the book in the car.

4. The sweater has shrank.

5. The last basket was thrown too late.

6. The pipes on the north side of the house have bursted.

7. Last night my tools were stole.

8. Has the girl sang professionally before?

9. The team members had swum fifty laps.

10. He done the work for us.

11. The kids had drank all of the fruit juice.

12. Had you saw the man in the lobby?

SKILL TEST

- Number your paper from 1 to 10.
- If a sentence has no errors in verb forms, write **C** after the corresponding number.
- If a sentence contains an incorrect verb form, rewrite the sentence correcting the error.

1. He drug the plow to the barn.

2. The whistles blew at eleven o'clock last Friday.

3. The bell had rang early this morning.

4. Were you given a good raise this year?

5. The cowhands have rode to the neighbor's ranch.

6. Had the child ever knowed his grandmother?

7. Last night I begun my paper for English.

8. She sung several songs for us.

9. The balloon bursted instantly.

10. I have seen that movie three times.

REVIEW A

- Write the sentences below. Underline and label the verb or verb phrase in each main clause; label the subject and any complements.
- Place parentheses around prepositional phrases.
- Draw a broken line beneath all phrases and clauses used as adjectives; identify each appropriately and draw an arrow to the word modified. Punctuate where necessary.

1. The game that he played last night is one that he will remember.

2. Naomi who had lost her ticket to the game sat outside dejectedly.

3. The man to watch this season is the end on Alabama's team.

4. The neon lights on the front of the building produced an effect that rivaled the sights of Las Vegas.

5. Raising the shade she saw the first rays of the sun peeping over the hill.

6. Pat Yen a rising political figure in Tulsa seems extremely capable.

7. An extremely talented young athlete who is willing to work hard can get educational assistance.

SKILL 4

Separating Troublesome Verb Pairs

Two words that are difficult to separate in meaning and use are the verbs lay and lie. Their differences, however, are distinguishable if studied carefully and separately.

The verb *lay* means to put or place. Study the examples below.

DO

They   lay   the tiles diagonally.
    (place)

DO

I lay the pattern on the material carefully.
(put)

The forms of the verb lay are as follows:

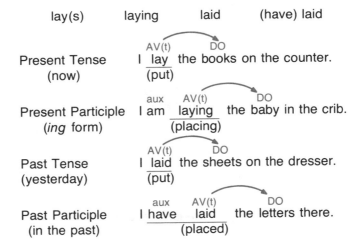

| | lay(s) | laying | laid | (have) laid |

Present Tense
(now)

AV(t)   DO
I lay the books on the counter.
(put)

Present Participle
(*ing* form)

aux   AV(t)   DO
I am laying the baby in the crib.
(placing)

Past Tense
(yesterday)

AV(t)   DO
I laid the sheets on the dresser.
(put)

Past Participle
(in the past)

aux   AV(t)   DO
I have laid the letters there.
(placed)

IMPORTANT

Note in the previous sentences that lay is a transitive verb. When used in any of its forms, it is always followed by a direct object.

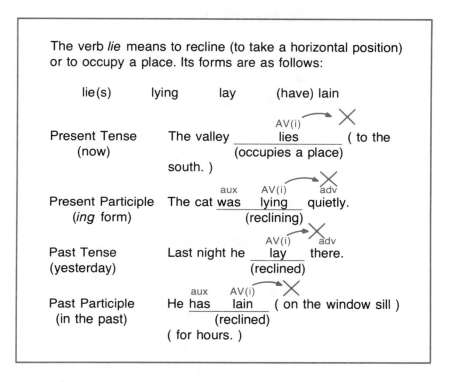

The verb *lie* means to recline (to take a horizontal position) or to occupy a place. Its forms are as follows:

lie(s)   lying   lay   (have) lain

Present Tense (now)   The valley ____lies____ (to the
                                                          (occupies a place)
                           south.)

Present Participle (*ing* form)   The cat was lying quietly.
                                                          (reclining)

Past Tense (yesterday)   Last night he lay there.
                                                          (reclined)

Past Participle (in the past)   He has lain (on the window sill)
                                                          (reclined)
                                     (for hours.)

IMPORTANT

Note in the sentences above that lie is an intransitive verb. It is never followed by a direct object.

Since lay is a form of both lie and lay, careful attention must be given to the tense and meaning required in the sentence.

Other troublesome verb pairs are set and sit, raise and rise. Like lie and lay, the words in each pair differ from each other in meaning. Also, like lie and lay, one in each pair is transitive and one is intransitive. Study the examples below.

The verb *set* means to place.

Present Tense
(now)

Usually we __set__ the vase in the middle.
AV(t) → DO
(place)

Present Participle
(*ing* form)

He is __setting__ the chairs in the living room.
aux AV(t) → DO
(placing)

Past Tense
(yesterday)

This morning she __set__ the plants outside.
AV(t) → DO
(placed)

Past Participle
(in the past)

The man had __set__ the package near the door.
aux AV(t) → DO
(placed)

Note above that the verb <u>set</u> is the <u>transitive</u> verb. It is <u>always</u> followed by a <u>direct object</u>.

The verb *sit* means to rest, to have or take a seat.

Present Tense
(now)

I __sit__ in the front row.
AV(i) ✗
(have a seat)

Present Participle
(*ing* form)

The box was __sitting__ here.
aux AV(i) ✗
(resting)

Past Tense
(yesterday)

The patient __sat__ nervously.
AV(i) ✗
(rested)

Past Participle
(in the past)

He __had sat__ on the fifty yard line.
aux AV(i) ✗
(took a seat)

Note that the verb <u>sit</u> is <u>intransitive</u>. It is <u>never followed</u> by a <u>direct object</u>.

The verb *raise* means to lift up, to push or put up.

Present Tense
(now)

They raise the flag at six.
(lift)
AV(t)   DO

Present Participle
(*ing* form)

The city is raising the property tax.
(pushing up)
aux   AV(t)   DO

Past Tense
(yesterday)

He raised his hand several times.
(lifted)
AV(t)   DO

Past Participle
(in the past)

She had raised the window.
(pushed up)
aux   AV(t)   DO

Note that the verb raise is transitive. It is always followed by a direct object.

The verb *rise* means to go up, to get up.

Present Tense
(now)
Each morning I ___rise___ at seven.
AV(i)
(get up)

Present Participle
(*ing* form)
The flood waters are ___rising___ slowly.
aux   AV(i)
(going up)

Past Tense
(yesterday)
The audience ___rose___ to its feet.
AV(i)
(got up)

Past Participle
(in the past)
The prices had ___risen___ dramatically.
aux   AV(i)
(gone up)

Note that the verb rise is intransitive. It is never followed by a direct object.

CHECKUP

Answer the following questions on a sheet of paper.

1. What are the definitions of the verbs lay and lie?
2. Which of these two verbs is transitive and which is intransitive?
3. What are the forms of lay and lie?
4. What are the definitions of the verbs set and sit?
5. Which of these two verbs is transitive and which is intransitive?
6. What are the forms of set and sit?
7. What are the definitions of the verbs raise and rise?
8. Which of these two verbs is transitive and which is intransitive?
9. What are the forms of raise and rise?

■ On a separate sheet follow the instructions below.

1. List the four forms of the verb lay.

2. Write the two meanings of the verb lay.

3. Write the following sentences, filling in the form of the verb lay as indicated. Label the principal parts; circle the direct object. Beneath each verb write its meaning. (Label the verb transitive.)

Present Tense   **a.** ____ the towels on this shelf.
                     (   )

Present Participle   **b.** They are ____ the bricks now.
                            (   )

Past Tense   **c.** After dinner Mom ____ the list here.
                            (   )

Past Participle   **d.** He had ____ his suit on the bed.
                        (   )

4. Follow the instructions for number 3. In addition, after each sentence write the tense of the verb required.

     a. Last night I ____ the task aside.
         (   )

     b. The waiter had already ____ the check on the table.
                (   )

     c. Then she ____ her tools in the garage.
          (   )

     d. ____ your paper on my desk.
      (   )

     e. They were ____ their wet swimsuits on the furniture.
          (   )

     f. Where has he ____ his glasses?
         (   )

     g. Always ____ it on the bottom.
        (   )

     h. The workers are ____ the carpet in the living room.
          (   )

     i. Later Aunt Vera ____ her purse here on the sofa.
          (   )

     j. The boys have ____ the logs near the fireplace.
         (   )

B

■ On a separate sheet follow the instructions below.

1. List the four forms of the verb lie.

2. Write the two meanings of the verb lie.

3. Write the sentences below, filling in the form of the verb indicated. Label all principal parts. Beneath each verb write its meaning. (Label the verb intransitive.)

Present Tense   **a.** _____ here on the couch.
( )

Present Participle   **b.** The vegetables are _____ in the sink.
( )

Past Tense   **c.** The victim _____ in the hospital for
( )
weeks.

Past Participle   **d.** Rover has _____ under the orange tree
( )
all day.

4. Follow the instructions for number 3. In addition, after each sentence, write the tense of the verb required.

a. Tabby _____ on the neighbor's roof for hours yesterday.
( )

b. The patient is _____ quietly now.
( )

c. He _____ down for a short nap every afternoon.
( )

d. At that time the camps _____ in the southern part of the state.
( )

e. The victim had _____ in the alley for several hours.
( )

f. Last week the boxes _____ in the warehouse.
( )

g. The oranges had been _____ on the ground.
( )

h. _____ down immediately.
( )

i. The pictures have _____ in the old chest for twenty years.
( )

j. After the phone call, she _____ awake until morning.
( )

■ On a separate sheet write the sentences below, leaving a blank for the verb.

■ After each sentence, write the tense of the verb required.

■ Beneath each blank in the sentence, write the meaning of the verb required.

■ Fill in the blanks with the proper forms of the verbs <u>lay</u> and <u>lie</u>.

■ Label the principal parts.

■ Label the verb transitive or intransitive.

1. At the last track meet, the contest _____ between you and me.
( )

2. The watch had _____ under the snow all winter.
( )

3. The neighbor had _____ the letter in our mailbox.
( )

4. Last night your keys _____ here on the dresser.
( )

5. Our morning newspaper was _____ on the roof of our next-door neighbor's garage.
( )

6. The answer _____ somewhere in this room.
( )

7. At school they now _____ their books on the lawn.
( )

8. After the meeting Mr. Norton _____ his complaint before the group.
( )

9. The building contract has _____ on your desk since early Monday afternoon.
( )

10. Father now _____ the blame on me.
( )

11. My younger sister Julie has been _____ her cheerleading clothes on my bed.
( )

12. They still _____ in the top drawer of the desk.
( )

13. The faded and water marked map had _____ in the sea chest for almost a century.
( )

D

■ On your paper write the correct verb.
■ Beneath each verb write its meaning.
■ Label the verb transitive or intransitive.

1. I saw the wrench (**laying / lying**) on the fender.
   (   )

2. The child was told to (**lay / lie**) quietly.
   (   )

3. The island (**lays / lies**) off the coast of Spain.
   (   )

4. The gunman (**laid / lay**) his guns on the marshall's desk.
   (   )

5. I noticed Craig (**laying / lying**) his books on the bench.
   (   )

6. Usually the maid (**lays / lies**) the articles in this drawer.
   (   )

7. My son had not (**laid / lain**) the mail in its usual place.
   (   )

8. Barbara (**laid / lay**) the gift on the bed and tiptoed out.
   (   )

9. For days after the incident, she (**laid / lay**) without sleeping.
   (   )

10. I had (**laid / lain**) in bed all day with a cold.
    (   )

11. Some (**lay / lie**) their jackets on the lawn and forget them.
    (   )

12. Pieces of the wreckage were (**lying / laying**) along the beach.
    (   )

E

■ On a separate sheet follow the directions below.

1. List the four forms of the verb <u>set</u>.

2. Write the meaning of the verb <u>set</u>.

3. Write the four sentences below, filling in the form of the verb indicated. Label the principal parts. Beneath each verb write its meaning. (Label the verb transitive.)

Present Tense   **a.** _____ the grocery bags on the counter.
(   )

Present Participle   **b.** Mother was already _____ the food on
(   )
the table.

Past Tense   **c.** Last night I _____ my wallet on the
(   )
nightstand.

Past Participle   **d.** The boy had _____ his racket on the
(   )
top of this.

1. List the four forms of the verb <u>sit</u>.

2. Write the two meanings of the verb <u>sit</u>.

3. Write the four sentences below, filling in the form of the verb indicated. Label the principal parts. Beneath each verb write its meaning. (Label the verb intransitive.)

Present Tense   **a.** Her father always _____ beside her.
(   )

Present Participle   **b.** The cat is _____ in her lap.
(   )

Past Tense   **c.** I _____ in this same seat yesterday.
(   )

Past Participle   **d.** Unfortunately he had _____ on the
(   )
fragile package.

F

■ On your paper write the correct verb.
■ Beneath each verb write its meaning.
■ Label the verb transitive or intransitive.

1. I (**sit** / **set**) in the first row.
(   )

2. The client had (**sat** / **set**) patiently for several hours.
(   )

3. Where were the guests (**sitting** / **setting**)?
(   )

4. At the last game I (**sat / set**) on the other side of the stadium.
   (   )

5. We have been (**sitting / setting**) the boxes under the counter.
   (   )

6. (**Sit / Set**) the lamp on this table.
   (   )

7. Who (**sits / sets**) here?
   (   )

8. The movers are (**sitting / setting**) the piano in the living room.
   (   )

9. Can the baby (**sit / set**) up by himself?
   (   )

10. I will (**sit / set**) the gifts in the bedroom.
    (   )

11. (**Sit / Set**) down for a few minutes.
    (   )

12. Last night I (**sat / set**) the contract on this table.
    (   )

G

■ On a separate sheet follow the directions below.

1. List the four forms of the verb <u>raise</u>.

2. Write the two meanings of the verb <u>raise</u>.

3. Write the four sentences below, filling in the form of the verb indicated. Label all principal parts. Beneath each verb write its meaning. (Label the verb transitive.)

Present Tense   a. _____ your right hand.
                               (   )

Present Participle   b. I am _____ the window.
                               (   )

Past Tense   c. Yesterday at the meeting, he _____
                                                   (   )
                 several objections.

Past Participle   d. You have _____ the curtain too soon.
                               (   )

1. List the four forms of the verb <u>rise</u>.

2. Write the two meanings of the verb <u>rise</u>.

3. Write the four sentences below, filling in the form of the verb indicated. Label all principal parts. Beneath each verb write its meaning. (Label the verb intransitive.)

Present Tense   **a.** He usually _____ around six.
                                      (   )

Present Participle   **b.** The bread was _____ slowly.
                                         (   )

Past Tense   **c.** The audience _____ to its feet.
                                       (   )

Past Participle   **d.** The sun had already _____.
                                       (   )

■ On your paper write the correct verb.
■ Beneath each verb write its meaning.
■ Label the verb transitive or intransitive.

1. The floods (**raised / rose**) the price of lettuce.
           (   )

2. Margaret often (**set / sat**) in a rocking chair on the porch.
           (   )

3. (**Set / Sit**) here near me.
    (   )

4. The moon (**rose / raised**) serenely over the bay.
           (   )

5. Mom had (**set / sat**) the hot pies on the patio table.
           (   )

6. The curtain (**rises / raises**) at eight.
           (   )

7. The rivers are (**rising / raising**) rapidly.
           (   )

8. The boys were (**setting / sitting**) on a bench near the library.
           (   )

9. The measure has (**raised / risen**) taxes.
           (   )

10. **(Set / Sit)** the boxes in the workroom.
   (   )

11. The workmen are **(sitting / setting)** the shrubs in today.
   (   )

12. Prices have **(raised / risen)** considerably this year.
   (   )

■ On your paper write the correct verb.
■ Beneath each verb write its meaning.
■ Label the verb transitive or intransitive.

1. The cleaner **(lay / laid)** the gown across the counter.
   (   )

2. **(Set / Sit)** the punchbowl on this end.
   (   )

3. The newspaper was **(laying / lying)** in the flower bed.
   (   )

4. She has **(raised / risen)** rapidly in the company.
   (   )

5. The men have **(laid / lain)** new carpet in the den.
   (   )

6. Where is he **(sitting / setting)**?
   (   )

7. The hotels **(raise / rise)** the prices during summer season.
   (   )

8. Some students were **(sitting / setting)** the chairs in place.
   (   )

9. The baby **(lay / laid)** quietly during the ceremony.
   (   )

10. Shakespeare had **(set / sat)** at this desk.
   (   )

11. Many are **(raising / rising)** their voices in protest.
   (   )

SKILL TEST

■ Number your paper from 1 to 10. Choose the correct verb in each sentence and write it beside the corresponding number.
■ Label each verb transitive or intransitive.

1. She had (**laid** / **lain**) her package on the bench beside her.

2. (**Set** / **Sit**) the butter dish on the table.

3. The dogs are (**laying** / **lying**) in the shade.

4. Who is (**setting** / **sitting**) near him?

5. Last night he (**lay** / **laid**) with a high fever.

6. Our hopes (**raised** / **rose**) for a few moments during the third quarter.

7. Yesterday I (**sat** / **set**) in the library during the afternoon.

8. (**Lie** / **Lay**) down and rest awhile.

9. Workers were (**rising** / **raising**) a scaffold on the front of the building.

10. (**Raise** / **Rise**) your hand before speaking.

REVIEW A

■ Underline and label the verb or verb phrase in each main clause below; label the subject and complement in each.
■ Draw a double line beneath any adverb structure—phrase or clause. Indicate the question each answers. Draw an arrow to the word modified. Indicate the subject and verb in the adverb clause.
■ Punctuate where necessary.

1. After she graduated from college she taught in Atlanta.

2. The audience soon grew restless because the speech was delivered in a monotone.

3. I can't go unless I earn two hundred dollars.

4. Although the Scotsman spoke English he was shy.

5. She lived in Detroit before automobiles were manufactured there.

6. At the explosion site on the Italian coast many leaped into the sea to escape the flames.

7. To insure one's future one should save in a systematic way.

8. We are going to Spain when this semester ends.

SKILL 5

Writing Sentences in Active and Passive Voice

In most sentences with action verbs, a subject <u>performs</u> the action and a direct object <u>receives</u> the action of the verb. Note the example below.

n(S) →AV(t) →n(DO)
Claudia <u>read</u> a story.

A sentence, such as the above, can be reversed by making the direct object the subject.

n(S)←aux   AV←————OP
A story <u>was read</u> (by Claudia).

When the subject performs the action of the verb, the sentence is said to be in the *active voice.*

When the sentence is reversed and the direct object becomes the subject, the subject no longer performs the action of the verb (it still receives). Such sentences are said to be in the *passive* (inactive) *voice.* Study the examples below.

                          S   AV   DO
Active Voice   Bob <u>ate</u> the pie.   (<u>Bob</u>, the subject, did
                                                          the eating.)

                          S   aux   AV   OP
Passive Voice   The pie <u>was eaten</u> (by Bob.)
                                                   (<u>Pie</u>, the subject, did
                                                     not do the eating.)

A sentence in the passive voice also has the following characteristics:

1. It always contains an <u>auxiliary verb</u>.
2. The original subject either appears in a <u>prepositional phrase</u> that begins with the preposition *by* or is entirely <u>omitted</u>.

Study the examples below.

Active Voice   A newspaper <u>published</u> the story.

n(S)   AV   n(DO)

Passive Voice   The story <u>was published</u> (by the

n(S)   aux   AV   p

n(OP)

newspaper.)

Passive Voice   The story <u>was published</u>.

n(S)   aux   AV

(Original subject has been omitted.)

When a sentence in active voice contains both a <u>direct object</u> and an <u>indirect object</u>, two passive forms are possible. Study the examples below.

Active Voice   Aaron <u>has written</u> me a letter.

n(S)   aux   AV   IO   DO

Passive Voice   I <u>was written</u> a letter by Aaron.

S   aux   AV

Passive Voice   A letter <u>was written</u> (to me) (by Aaron.)

S   aux   AV   p   OP   p   OP

IMPORTANT

Remember that when a pronoun changes its function, it often changes in form, nominative to objective or objective to nominative. Note below.

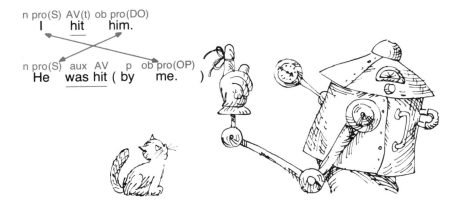

n pro(S) AV(t) ob pro(DO)
  I   hit   him.

n pro(S) aux AV   p ob pro(OP)
He was hit (by   me.)

CHECKUP

Answer the following questions on a separate sheet of paper.

1. When is a sentence in the active voice?
2. When is a sentence in the passive voice?
3. How can a sentence be changed from the active to the passive voice?
4. When does a sentence have two passive forms?

A

■ On a separate sheet change the following sentences from active to passive voice by making the direct object the subject, adding an auxiliary verb (a form of *be*), and placing the original subject in a prepositional phrase that begins with the preposition *by*.

■ Refer back to the symbols ⌐ and ☐ if you need help.

1. The school board hired me.
2. My parents have bought a new car.
3. The audience loves his jokes.
4. She studied the situation carefully.
5. The Yankees won the series.
6. Some appreciate them.
7. Who forgot it?

B

■ On a separate sheet change the following sentences from active to passive voice omitting the original subject.

■ Refer back to the symbols ☐, ☐, and ☐☐ if you need help.

1. Many celebrated the victory.
2. Everyone will remember his name.
3. The officials cancelled the game.
4. Someone made a mistake.
5. The client has withdrawn her offer.
6. The station didn't announce the winner.
7. It amazes everyone.

C

■ On a separate sheet rewrite each active voice sentence below in its two passive forms, using first the direct object as the subject and then the indirect object.

■ Refer back to the symbols ⊞ and ☐ if you need help.

1. The teacher gave us a hard exam.
2. The company paid the investors a dividend.
3. An unknown admirer sends my sister flowers.
4. She has taught him the business.
5. The owner has probably told you the procedure.
6. Who gave him the idea?

D

■ Number your paper from 1 to 12.
■ Decide in which voice each sentence below is written (active or passive), and write your answer beside the corresponding number.

1. A note was handed him by a messenger.
2. The luggage is tagged immediately.

3. Some areas of the valley were flooded.

4. My brother and your sister eloped yesterday.

5. His parents bought him a new wardrobe.

6. The school has been closed for repair.

7. Rita tells me everything.

8. He has been appointed chairperson by the firm's president.

9. The queen was given the ruby by a royal visitor.

10. Our coach has played professional baseball.

11. The fly ball was caught by the centerfielder.

12. The yearbook will be published in April.

SKILL TEST

■ Number your paper from 1 to 10.
■ Decide in which voice each sentence below is written (active or passive), and write your answer beside the corresponding number.

1. The program is sponsored by several companies.

2. The foreman had managed the ranch well.

3. The stadium was filled to capacity.

4. The investors had been convinced of the project's eventual success.

5. The store always gives the employees a discount.

6. He has been repaying the loan for many years.

7. My Aunt Helen was educated at Vassar.

8. The dock workers are striking for higher wages.

9. The error had been made in the original order.

10. She was given a severe reprimand by the judge.

REVIEW A

■ Number your paper from 1 to 10.

■ Beside the corresponding number, write the subject of each sentence below.

■ Indicate whether the subject is singular or plural by writing a **1** or **2** above it.

■ After each subject choose the verb that agrees with it in number; write a **1** or **2** above it indicating singular or plural.

■ Check to see if the subject and verb in each sentence agree in number.

1. (**Has** / **Have**) the crowd dispersed yet?

2. (**Here's** / **Here are**) the latest details.

3. A member of one of the teams (**speaks** / **speak**) Japanese.

4. Other copies of the manuscript (**was** / **were**) lost.

5. Where (**is** / **are**) the stuffed elephants?

6. (**Doesn't** / **Don't**) your brother have a motorcycle?

7. (**Is** / **Are**) each ready for shipment?

8. Many in the class (**participates** / **participate**) in extracurricular activity.

9. Either (**is** / **are**) acceptable.

10. This (**don't** / **doesn't**) count.

REVIEW B

■ On a separate sheet beside the corresponding number, write the subject or subjects in each sentence below and any conjunctions that connect them.

■ Indicate whether each subject is singular or plural by writing a **1** or **2** above it.

■ Note carefully the conjunctions used; then after the subject(s), choose the verb that agrees in number. Write a **1** or **2** above it.

■ Check carefully to see if the subject(s) and verb agree.

1. Some grapes or an apple (**was** / **were**) provided for a snack.

2. The girls, along with their chaperone, (**has** / **have**) been given special invitations.

3. Either baking soda or buttermilk (**is** / **are**) used in the cornbread.

Correct Verb Usage

4. Both the coaches and the pitcher (**lives** / **live**) in Phoenix.

5. Several like this one (**is** / **are**) found near San Diego.

6. (**There's** / **There are**) pie or custard for dessert.

7. Neither he nor they (**enjoys** / **enjoy**) golf.

8. (**Where's** / **Where are**) the wrapping paper and ribbons?

REVIEW C

■ Number your paper from 1 to 10.
■ If a sentence has no errors in verb forms, write **C** after the corresponding number on your paper.
■ If a sentence contains an incorrect verb form, rewrite the sentence correcting the error.

1. Some had brung their baseball gear to the picnic.

2. She throwed three strikes in a row.

3. The family has written the invitations already.

4. I have ran the mile in less than five minutes.

5. Several women have now swam the English Channel.

6. The sixth period bell rung ten minutes ago.

7. The gardener done a very good job for us.

8. Last night the pipes burst from the cold weather.

9. Have you ever saw a prettier one?

10. You haven't drunk your milk.

REVIEW D

■ Number your paper from 1 to 10.
■ Choose the correct verb in each sentence and write it beside the corresponding number.
■ Label each verb transitive or intransitive.

1. Her son had (**laid** / **lain**) the keys in her desk drawer.

2. He usually (**sets** / **sits**) the milk here on the front steps.

3. The team's spirit has (**risen** / **raised**) considerably.

4. Noreen (**set** / **sat**) the plates on the bar.

5. Who is (**lying** / **laying**) in the hammock?

6. The retailers will (**raise** / **rise**) the price of beef again this month.

7. She (**lay** / **laid**) in the sun too long.

8. The vice-president is (**setting** / **sitting**) beside her.

9. (**Raise** / **Rise**) early!

10. (**Lay** / **Lie**) the napkins on the left side of the plate.

REVIEW E

■ Study the verb or verb phrase in each sentence below for correct form, correct meaning, and number agreement with the subject(s).
■ Number your paper from 1 to 15.
■ If the verb in the sentence is used correctly, write a **C** beside the corresponding number.
■ If the verb is incorrectly used, rewrite the sentence correcting the error.

1. Last year I set behind her.

2. Our grocer has raised the prices of many foods.

3. Neither the students nor the teacher feels good about this program.

4. Your mail and your package is being forwarded to your new address.

5. She had lain her briefcase on the seat beside her.

6. Either Allan or my parents is bringing the cake.

7. Each of the many paintings have been carefully cleaned.

8. I haven't swum in three years.

9. Mr. Ruiz, together with his students, have planned a book fair.

10. As a girl she had stole bread for her family.

11. Here's the two best specimens.

12. My brother sung several songs at her wedding.

13. Neither Kim, Serene, nor Catherine are eligible to play in the game tonight.

14. Then you lay the chicken into the hot oil.

15. Aren't the refreshments ready?

REVIEW F

- Number your paper from 1 to 10.
- Decide in which voice each sentence below is written (active or passive), and write your answer beside the corresponding number.

1. The situation in the Middle East is being watched carefully.

2. The verdict surprised everyone.

3. Her boss has given her a two-weeks paid vacation.

4. What happened?

5. His tapes have been purchased by millions of teenagers.

6. Our team has been winning consistently.

7. Many good ideas for improving attendance were presented at the last meeting.

8. Some in the group have complained to the airlines about their difficulties.

9. My parents disapprove of the entire idea.

10. The land swindler was given a stiff sentence by Judge Simpson.

GRAMMAR

STEP-BY-STEP

UNIT VII

Correct Pronoun Usage

UNIT VII

Correct Pronoun Usage

SKILL 1

Making Pronouns Agree with Antecedents

A <u>pronoun</u> serves as a <u>substitute</u> for a <u>noun</u>. Note below.

(Ross) left early; (Ross) was ill.

(Ross) left early; (he) was ill.

Noun ◄───── Pronoun (noun substitute)

The noun to which the pronoun refers is called the pronoun's *antecedent* (that which logically comes before).

n(S)
The (members) of the group have pledged (their) support.

Antecedent ◄─────────────── Pronoun

n(S)
The (invention) has proved (its) worth.

Antecedent   Pronoun

| The noun to which a pronoun refers should always <u>precede</u> the pronoun. Note below.

Wrong

In (his) business dealings, (Mr. Ferrino) is always extremely fair.

Pronoun ─✗─✗─✗─✗─► Noun

Right

(Mr. Ferrino) is always extremely fair in (his) business dealings.

Noun   ◄─────────────── Pronoun
Antecedent

|| Indefinite pronouns can also serve as antecedents. Note below.

id pro(S)   ps pro

(Everyone) brought (her) own equipment.

Antecedent ← Pronoun

(S)
id pro   ob pro(DO)

(All) sat quietly; the news had stunned (them).

Antecedent ← Pronoun

Just as a verb must agree with the subject in number, a pronoun must agree with its antecedent in number. Note below.

1   1
n(S)   ps pro

The (professor) devoted (his) life to music.

Antecedent ← Pronoun

Singular = Singular

2   2
n(S)   n pro(S)

The (animals) were out; (they) had dug a hole under the fence.

Antecedent ← Pronoun

Plural = Plural

A pronoun can have more than one antecedent. Note below that when antecedents are connected by the conjunction *and,* the pronoun is plural.

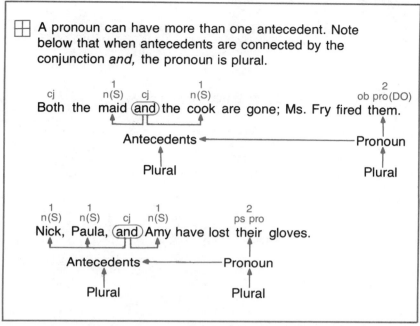

When antecedents are connected by the conjunction *or* or the conjunction pairs *either . . . or* or *neither . . . nor,* the pronoun that follows agrees in number with the closest antecedent. Note below.

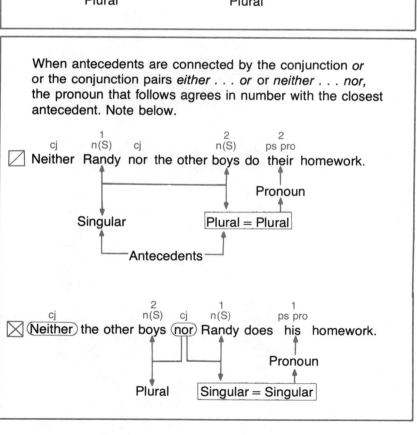

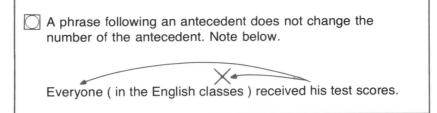

○ A phrase following an antecedent does not change the number of the antecedent. Note below.

Everyone (in the English classes) received his test scores.

The number of pronouns is indicated below. A circle has been drawn around each singular pronoun and a box around each plural pronoun.

Nominative	**Objective**	**Possessive**
Ⓘ	ⓜⓔ (me)	(my)
(you)	(you)	(your)
(he) (she) (it)	(him) (her) (it)	(his) (her) (its)
we	us	our
you	you	your
they	them	their

Indefinite Pronouns

*any	(anyone)	(anybody)	(anything)
(each)	(everyone)	(everybody)	(everything)
*none	(no one)	(nobody)	(nothing)
*some	(someone)	(somebody)	(something)

few		(one)
several		(other)
many		(another)
*more		(either)
*most		(neither)
*all		both

Asterisks indicate pronouns that can be singular and plural.

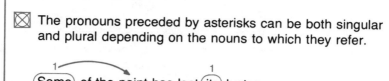

The pronouns preceded by asterisks can be both singular and plural depending on the nouns to which they refer.

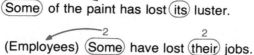

(Some) of the paint has lost (its) luster.

(Employees) (Some) have lost (their) jobs.

CHECKUP

Answer the following questions on a separate sheet of paper.

1. What is the position of a pronoun in relationship to its antecedent?
2. What is the meaning of the word *antecedent?*
3. What part of speech other than a noun can be an antecedent?
4. In what way must a pronoun agree with its antecedent?
5. When two antecedents are joined by *and,* the pronoun must be _____ in number.
6. When two antecedents are joined by *or* or *nor,* with which antecedent does the pronoun that follows agree in number?
7. Which 18 indefinite pronouns are singular?
8. Which 4 indefinite pronouns are plural?
9. Which 6 indefinite pronouns can be both singular and plural?

■ On a separate sheet write the sentences below.
■ Circle the pronoun and draw an arrow from it to its antecedent.

1. The little girl had spilled her crayons.
2. Every golfer on the course had his own set of clubs.
3. Many are nervous on their first day of school.
4. The football player had broken his finger.
5. The officer says that she recognized the suspect last night.
6. When the guests arrive, they will meet a strange host.
7. Has the cat been given its shots?
8. Some do not want to return; the memories bother them.
9. The car had a dent in its left rear fender.
10. Ed's parents want Ty to spend the day at their cabin with them.

A 2

■ On a separate sheet write the sentences below.
■ Circle the pronoun in each sentence and draw an arrow from it to its antecedent.

1. The long distance runner had left his opponents far behind and had dashed their hopes for first place.

2. The basketball coach wants the new players to report to him after their physicals.

3. The drama department is holding auditions for its spring play; they began yesterday.

4. Uncle Harold keeps his boat here but seldom uses it.

5. Several in the group had their fortunes told.

B

■ On a separate sheet rewrite the following sentences positioning each pronoun correctly in relationship to its antecedent.
■ Refer back to symbol | if you need help.

1. In her room Audrey found a baby rattlesnake.

2. When he realized that the new invention would help many people, the banker assured the inventor that he would receive financial support.

3. Shouldering his golf bag, the pro started off after his ball.

4. Because of her fear of air travel, Carolyn took the bus to Los Angeles.

5. Their great love for horses often interfered with the twins' studies.

6. It had been built in 1921, so the car was a valuable antique.

7. The clerk had overcharged them, but the children had not noticed.

8. Whenever he says he is going to do something, Leonard always does it.

9. As she cared for them, the nurse learned to love the patients.

10. Before they finished the story, most had decided that they liked it.

C

■ On your paper, separate the pronouns below into three columns labeled **Singular, Plural,** and **Either.**

he	all	this	any	several
neither	each	someone	its	their
nothing	hers	they	she	that
them	both	his	other	it
one	many	none	somebody	him
some	these	either	more	those
her	few	another	anyone	most

D

■ Number your paper from 1 to 6.
■ Decide which pronoun in the parentheses agrees in number with the antecedent.
■ Write the pronoun beside the corresponding number.
■ Refer back to symbol if you need help.

1. None of the sound had retained (**its** / **their**) clarity.

2. None of the students had done (**his** / **their**) assignment.

3. Some of the voters had registered (**his** / **their**) protest.

4. Some of the juice had lost (**its** / **their**) flavor.

5. Most of the trees had dropped (**its** / **their**) leaves.

6. Most of the portrait had been changed from (**its** / **their**) original color.

E

■ On a separate sheet beside the corresponding number, first write the antecedent.
■ Then choose the pronoun in the parentheses that agrees with the antecedent in number.
■ Use the symbols to refer back to examples on pages 254–257.

1. The gymnastics class is preparing for (**its** / **their**) exhibition before the student body.

2. Jennifer, one of my students, has broken (**their** / **her**) leg.

3. Will some be driving (**his** / **their**) cars to Daytona Saturday?

4. Each of the officers found (**his** / **their**) own place card at the table.

5. Nobody in the class is so smart that (**he** / **they**) cannot benefit from the teacher's help.

6. Each candidate presented (**his** / **their**) views on the subject.

7. The officers were accompanied by (**her** / **their**) husbands.

8. When one visits the Grand Canyon, (**he is** / **they are**) awed by its grandeur.

9. At the officers' banquet, everyone was seated according to (**his** / **their**) military rank.

10. A few of the fans had brought (**his** / **their**) own cushions.

11. None of the oil had escaped from (**its** / **their**) container.

12. None of the students realized (**his** / **their**) potential.

F

■ On a separate sheet beside the corresponding number, write the antecedent or antecedents and any conjunctions that connect them.
■ After the antecedent(s) write the pronoun in the parentheses that agrees in number.
■ Use the symbols to refer back to examples on pages 254–257.

1. Neither Harold nor Bert felt that (**his** / **their**) time at the library was well spent.

2. Either Helen, Terri, or Elaine will have to change (**their** / **her**) schedule.

3. My son James and his friend Steve packed (**their** / **his**) camping equipment into the van.

4. Either the pickup or the car always had (**their** / **its**) gas tank empty.

5. Neither Robert nor the other boys had completed (**their** / **his**) chores.

6. Either the girls or Donald will be ready to read (**their** / **his**) essay in the contest.

7. Anita, Robin, and Jason made (**their** / **her** / **his**) own rocket model.

8. Neither Vincent nor his partners would discuss (**his** / **their**) business with anyone.

9. An athlete or band member should advise (**his** / **their**) parents when extra practices are scheduled.

10. Some of the cheerleaders or the student council will offer (**their** / **its**) help to the project.

G

■ On a separate sheet beside the corresponding number, write the pronoun in the parentheses that agrees with the antecedents in number.

■ Use the symbols to check your answers.

1. Both my son and my daughter will be awarded (**their** / **his** / **her**) diplomas this week.

2. The cars had (**their** / **its**) tires replaced yesterday.

3. Several in the group had worn (**their** / **his**) tennis shoes.

4. Each of the classes had been assigned to (**their** / **its**) homeroom.

5. Neither the Buick nor the Pontiac had been given (**their** / **its**) final coat of paint.

6. None of the boys could find (**their** / **his**) hiking boots.

7. Janet and Iris will bring (**their** / **her**) special projects to class tomorrow.

8. Everyone can have (**their** / **her**) own gym locker.

9. All will have to return (**their** / **his**) books.

10. Neither Debbie nor her parents had purchased (**her** / **their**) tickets yet.

11. Some of the fruit had lost (**its** / **their**) flavor.

12. Either the players or the coach will have to change (**her** / **their**) schedules.

SKILL TEST

On a separate sheet beside the corresponding number, write the pronoun found in the parentheses that agrees with the antecedent(s) in number.

1. Both Leo and Tom will give you (**his** / **their**) report.

2. Each of the contestants did (**her** / **their**) very best.

3. Either Betty or June left (**their** / **her**) books in my car.

4. Most of the forest had lost (**their** / **its**) foliage.

5. Neither the fielders nor the catcher thought the error (**his** / **theirs**).

6. One of the boys had (**his** / **their**) paintings accepted for display.

7. If one of the levers had broken, (**it** / **they**) would have caused the death of many workers.

8. Everybody in the drama class had already purchased (**his** / **their**) ticket.

9. Neither of the mothers could recognize (**their** / **her**) children's faults.

10. Anyone who writes a book knows (**they** / **he**) will spend many hours alone.

REVIEW A

■ On a separate sheet write the sentences below choosing the correct pronoun(s).
■ Label all words in the sentence.

1. **a.** Sandy, Theresa, and (**us** / **we**) are going to the game tonight.

   b. (**Them** / **They**), my brother, and (**I** / **me**) were chosen for the team.

2. **a.** The finalists are (**he** / **him**) and (**me** / **I**).

   b. The best ones had been (**them** / **they**) or (**we** / **us**).

3. **a.** The group gave (**she** / **her**) and (**he** / **him**) an award.

   b. The audience likes both (**they** / **them**) and (**me** / **I**).

4. **a.** Denise wrote to (**him** / **he**) and (**me** / **I**).

   b. The bus left without either (**them** / **they**) or (**she** / **her**).

REVIEW B

■ On a separate sheet write the sentences below replacing any incorrect pronoun with the correct form.
■ Label all words in the sentence.

1. He and her will graduate this year.

2. The teacher encouraged them and I.

3. The trophy was presented by him and us.

4. The best performers were you and her.

5. Them and us will be in the tennis finals.

SKILL 2

Avoiding Ambiguous Pronouns

A pronoun is *ambiguous* when it does not have an antecedent to which it clearly refers.

An *ambiguity* (uncertainty or double meaning) occurs when an antecedent cannot be distinguished from other nouns that precede the pronoun. Study the examples below.

Unclear

After the coach talked with Gary, he left the gym.

Clear

The coach left the gym after he talked with Gary.

Unclear

When the truck collided with the van, it burst into flames.

Clear

The truck burst into flames when it collided with the van.

‖ Another error in pronoun usage that results in ambiguity is the use of a pronoun <u>without</u> an antecedent. Study the following examples:

Unclear

Many people who are heavy smokers are trying to stop (it).

——————————————— Pronoun

Clear

Many heavy smokers are trying to break the habit. (No pronoun)

Unclear

My parents are supporting the bill, (which) is a mistake.

——————————————— Pronoun

Clear

My parents' support of the bill is a mistake. (No pronoun)

Ambiguity also arises from the incorrect use of the pronouns *you* and *they.* These two pronouns should not be used when the meaning can be expressed with more precise words.

Imprecise

In the Middle Ages (you) were sometimes sentenced to death without trial.

Precise

In the Middle Ages (people) were sometimes sentenced to death without trial.

Imprecise

At our school (they) always serve nourishing lunches.

Precise

At our school (students) always receive nourishing lunches.

CHECKUP

Answer the following questions on a separate sheet of paper.

1. What is the meaning of the word *ambiguous?*
2. What are three types of ambiguities that arise from the incorrect use of pronouns?

A₁

■ Each sentence below contains an ambiguous pronoun. To understand the problem in each, use the symbols to refer to the examples on the previous pages.

■ On a separate sheet rewrite each sentence correcting the pronoun error.

1. When the Smiths return with the rolls, we'll pop them in the oven.
2. Many dislike turnips and rutabagas, which I can understand.
3. In some colonies you were a witch unless you could prove yourselves otherwise.

A 2

■ On your paper rewrite each sentence below correcting the pronoun error.

■ Before each sentence draw the symbol that represents the problem involved.

1. In Saudi Arabia they cut your hands off for stealing.

2. When Jill hurt Lorraine's feelings, I suggested that she ignore the whole episode.

3. The group doesn't want Ted to know about the plan because it would spoil the fun.

B

■ On a separate sheet rewrite each sentence below correcting the pronoun error.

■ Before each sentence draw the symbol that represents the problem involved.

1. As the plane hit the house, it exploded.

2. In Salt Lake City, they have a monument to seagulls.

3. Dad explained to Mark the consequences of his actions.

4. Most people find that it doesn't pay to take short cuts.

5. At the dance Sheila sang and danced, which everyone enjoyed.

6. In several recent articles, they have discussed the pros and cons of the issue.

7. Because the cat had been bitten by the dog, Dad had it put to sleep.

8. The circus is coming to town, which is exciting to my children.

C

■ On a separate sheet, number from 1 to 10.

■ Rewrite each sentence below that contains a problem in pronoun usage, correcting the error.

■ Place a **C** after the corresponding number if the sentence contains no errors.

1. When Mrs. Jones put the radish in my salad, I couldn't eat it.

2. Many in the stadium had brought their umbrellas.

3. If they want to win the tournament, the team members will have to be more diligent in their practice.

4. Neither the kids nor Dad did his part in getting ready for the reception.

5. When people are bored, it makes them sleepy.

6. Each of the children had brought their own sleeping bag.

7. When I was a kid, you just didn't do those things.

8. Both the cake and the punch had lost their flavor.

9. In the novel it tells about the struggle of one young man to understand himself.

10. Everybody in the group appreciated their free time during the afternoon.

■ Carefully check the use of pronouns in the sentences below. Watch for ambiguities in pronoun usage, the lack of agreement between pronouns and their antecedents, and incorrect positioning of pronouns in relation to their antecedents.

■ Number your paper from 1 to 10.

■ If the sentence contains no error, write **C** after the corresponding number.

■ After the other numbers, rewrite correctly those sentences that contain errors.

1. Both the stapler and the tape had been removed from its usual place.

2. One of the exotic snakes in the last row of glass cages had shed their beautiful skin.

3. Because of her asthma, Sherri has missed several school activities this year.

4. In ancient Greece you had to plead your own case before the public.

5. The director of our lunch programs must have given her permission for the change.

6. Every boy must make his contribution to the success of this team.

7. None of the school orchestra's fund-raising projects could have supported themselves.

8. The stockholders want to raise prices, but it would be a bad decision.

9. Neither the sponsor of the chess club nor its three officers should pay their own registration fee.

10. The scientist wrote several memos to the director of the institute about her findings.

SKILL TEST

■ Carefully check the use of pronouns in the sentences below. Watch for ambiguities in pronoun usage, the lack of agreement between pronouns and their antecedents, and incorrect positioning of pronouns in relation to their antecedents.
■ Number your paper from 1 to 10.
■ If the sentence contains no error, write **C** after the corresponding number.
■ After the other numbers, rewrite correctly those sentences that contain errors.

1. Everybody should be strong in their support of the new liquor laws.

2. Unfortunately, several of the cars in the parking lot on the west side of the building had its tires slashed.

3. Both the supervisor and his assistant could be assigned his own work area.

4. The principals at that school must have been especially dedicated to their responsibilities.

5. Most of the produce had lost their freshness.

6. Norman wanted to drive a group to the game last night, but his parents didn't approve of that.

7. Several times during their routine on the field, the pom pom girls were loudly applauded.

8. Either the cheerleaders or the pep squad could donate a few hours of their time.

9. In England they have their steering wheels on the opposite side of the car.

10. Judy tried to tell Martha how she would feel in the same situation.

REVIEW A

■ On a separate sheet beside the corresponding number, write the pronoun found in the parentheses that agrees with the antecedent(s) in number.

1. Every student should check with (**their** / **his**) own doctor.

2. Neither the teenager nor his parents returned to (**his** / **their**) home.

3. One should follow (**their** / **your** / **his**) aptitudes to success.

4. Neither the members of the chorus nor the director had finished (**his** / **their**) costume(s) for tonight's performance.

5. Everyone gave (**his** / **their**) complete support to the project.

6. Either the sponsor or the class officers had broken (**their** / **his**) promise to keep the secret.

7. Both Mr. Chang and the coach did not attend; (**he** / **they**) sent an apology.

8. Had each of the members of the team reported (**his** / **their**) expenses?

9. Some of the paint on the cars had lost (**its** / **their**) luster.

10. The congregation is planning (**their** / **its**) biggest fund raising event.

11. Anyone may turn in (**his** / **their**) equipment after two o'clock.

12. A few of the group forgot (**his** / **their**) canteens.

SKILL 3

Using *Who* and *Whom* Correctly

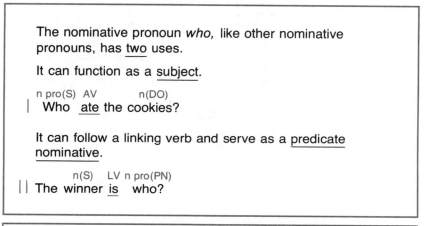

The nominative pronoun *who,* like other nominative pronouns, has <u>two</u> uses.

It can function as a <u>subject</u>.

```
 n pro(S)  AV        n(DO)
| Who  ate  the cookies?
```

It can follow a linking verb and serve as a <u>predicate nominative</u>.

```
        n(S)   LV n pro(PN)
|| The winner is   who?
```

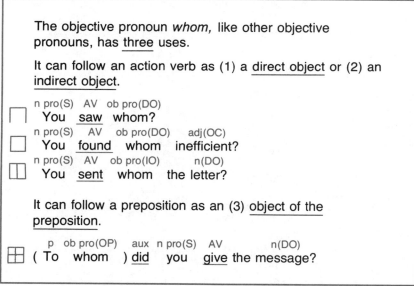

The objective pronoun *whom,* like other objective pronouns, has <u>three</u> uses.

It can follow an action verb as (1) a <u>direct object</u> or (2) an <u>indirect object</u>.

```
 n pro(S)  AV  ob pro(DO)
  You  saw  whom?
 n pro(S)   AV   ob pro(DO)    adj(OC)
  You  found  whom   inefficient?
 n pro(S)   AV  ob pro(IO)      n(DO)
  You  sent  whom   the letter?
```

It can follow a preposition as an (3) <u>object of the preposition</u>.

```
    p  ob pro(OP)  aux n pro(S)  AV        n(DO)
( To  whom  ) did  you  give the message?
```

IMPORTANT

An accurate choice between the pronouns *who* and *whom* can be made only after the function of the pronoun has been determined.

In some questions the order of the sentence parts is *inverted* (reversed). Changing such sentences into "natural" order helps in determining the function of the pronoun (subject, predicate nominative, direct object, etc.) and thereafter the correct choice of pronouns.

Who
(or)
Whom

n(S)
can the culprit be?

n(S)   aux LV   n pro(PN)
The culprit can be   who   ? ──→ Nominative pronouns follow linking verbs and serve as predicate nominatives.

Linking ──→ Predicate
Verb   Nominative

Who
(or)
Whom

n(S)
will the committee hire?

n(S)   aux AV   ob pro(DO)
The committee will hire   whom   ? ──→ Object pronouns follow action verbs and serve as direct objects.

Action ──→ Direct
Verb   Object

The same logic for the use of *who* and *whom* in a simple sentence applies to their use in a subordinate clause in a complex sentence.

⊠ *Who* can be the subject of a <u>subordinate clause</u>.

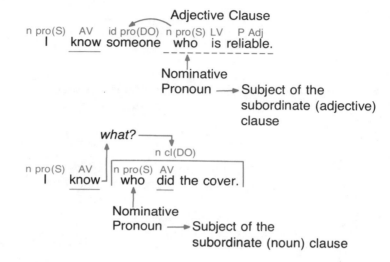

Who and whom usually serve as complements when the verb of the subordinate clause already has a subject. In such cases, the verb determines the function.

Rearranging the subordinate clause into "natural" order helps in determining the function of the pronoun. Note below.

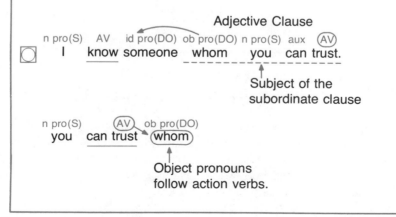

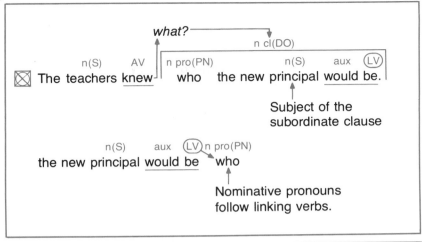

In an adjective clause *whom,* not *who,* follows a preposition as object of the preposition. Note below.

adjective clause

n(S)   p ob pro(OP)   s   v   LV   n(PN)
The man (to   whom   ) she is speaking is the composer.

Sometimes the object of the preposition *whom* is separated from the preposition.

adjective clause

n(S) ob pro(OP) s   v   p   LV   n(PN)
The man   whom   she is speaking to is the composer.

CHECKUP

Answer the following questions on a separate sheet of paper.

1. Which of the two pronouns, *who* or *whom,* is nominative? Which is objective?
2. What are the two uses of the pronoun *who?*
3. What are the three uses of the pronoun *whom?*
4. Which of the two can be the subject of a subordinate clause?
5. When a subordinate clause "already" has a subject, what usually determines the choice of pronouns?
6. Which pronoun always follows the preposition?

A

■ Number your paper from 1 to 5.
■ Beside the corresponding number, first write the function in the sentence of the pronoun needed. **(S, PN, DO, IO, OP)**
■ Then write the pronoun in the parentheses that can perform that function.
■ Use the symbols to refer back to the examples on pages 271–274 if help is needed.

 1. (**Who** / **Whom**) was the last holder of the title?
 2. The next speaker is (**who** / **whom**)?
 3. Dwight beat (**who** / **whom**)?
 4. She mailed (**who** / **whom**) the package?
 5. The supervisor thinks (**who** / **whom**) incapable?

 1. The last contestant will be (**who** / **whom**)?
 2. The club supported (**who** / **whom**)?
 3. (**Who** / **Whom**) ate the pies?
 4. The child gave the note to (**who** / **whom**)?
 5. They consider (**who** / **whom**) the best choice?

 1. The polls name (**who** / **whom**) the next president?
 2. (**Who** / **Whom**) broke the projector?
 3. You need a recommendation from (**who** / **whom**)?
 4. The victim was (**who** / **whom**)?
 5. Your brother married (**who** / **whom**)?

B

■ Before choosing the correct pronoun for each question below, rewrite each on your paper changing it into natural order. (Refer back to symbols ◻ and ◻ if you need help.)
■ Write the function of the pronoun after each sentence before inserting the correct pronoun.
■ Then write the original question using the correct pronoun.

1. **(Who / Whom)** will our spokesperson be?
2. **(Who / Whom)** did the committee select?
3. **(Who / Whom)** has your lawyer been in the past?
4. **(Who / Whom)** does the document designate?
5. **(Who / Whom)** did you send for the ice?
6. **(Who / Whom)** would her escort be?
7. To **(who / whom)** did he give the pen?
8. **(Who / Whom)** did they call a coward?
9. **(Who / Whom)** do you consider gifted?

C

■ Number your paper from 1 to 7.
■ Beside the corresponding number, first write the function in the sentence of the pronoun needed. **(S, PN, DO, IO, OP)**
■ Then write the pronoun in the parentheses that can perform that function.
■ Use the symbols to refer back to the examples on pages 271–274 if necessary.

1. **(Who / Whom)** had the supervisor fired?
2. **(Who / Whom)** are the best comics in television today?
3. **(Who / Whom)** hid the money?
4. Until that time **(who / whom)** had his favorite guitarist been?
5. **(Who / Whom)** will the student body elect?
6. **(Who / Whom)** might the stranger have been?
7. With **(who / whom)** did she leave?

□ **1.** **(Who / Whom)** could the mysterious caller have been?

❘ **2.** **(Who / Whom)** are the finalists?

⊠ **3.** **(Who / Whom)** would the students prefer?

□ **4.** **(Who / Whom)** should the narrator be?

⊠ **5.** **(Who / Whom)** did the judges choose?

❘ **6.** **(Who / Whom)** borrowed my brush?

⊞ **7.** For **(who / whom)** did you make the gift?

D

■ On your paper beside the corresponding number, copy the adjective clause in each sentence, carefully choosing the correct pronoun and labeling the principal parts of the clause.

■ If necessary refer to symbol on page 273.

■ Review the punctuation rules below the sentences.

1. Dewey Williams,* **(who / whom)** had requested a conference with the girl's parents,* placed her temporarily in study hall.

2. Hopefully the athlete **(who / whom)** becomes the winner of the decathlon will give us an interview.

3. A small, bald, inconspicuous man,** **(who / whom)** had been standing in the back of the room,** suddenly blew a whistle.

4. We consider him an engineer **(who / whom)** could solve any metallurgical problem.

5. My mother,*** **(who / whom)** was born in Florida,*** speaks like a Southerner.

*Remember that an adjective clause is considered nonessential and is separated from the rest of the sentence by commas when it modifies a proper noun.

**Remember that an adjective clause is also considered nonessential and is separated by commas when the noun modified is specifically identified by several modifiers that precede it.

***Remember that an adjective clause is also considered nonessential and is separated by commas when the noun modified is preceded by a possessive that specifically identifies it.

- Locate the adjective clause in each sentence below.
- Before choosing the correct pronoun for each, rewrite the clause on your paper changing it into natural order. (Refer to symbols ◯ and ⊠ if necessary.)
- Write the function of the pronoun after each clause before inserting the correct pronoun.
- Rewrite the original sentence inserting the correct pronoun.
- Label the principal parts of the main clause.
- Punctuate where necessary. (Review punctuation rules in the footnotes of the previous exercise.)

1. He was the man (**who** / **whom**) the committee selected.

2. The candidate (**who** / **whom**) I thought best qualified has dropped out of the race.

3. I then called Dr. Romero (**who** / **whom**) several friends had recommended.

4. The person (**who** / **whom**) she later becomes is bitter and arrogant.

5. The adorable, curly-haired child (**who** / **whom**) the social agency had sent them became the center of their existence.

6. The next king of England (**who** / **whom**) Prince Charles will someday be will be crowned like his predecessors in Westminster Abbey.

7. The bank finds her an employee (**who** / **whom**) it can trust implicitly.

8. The agency is sending us an experienced, bilingual, male secretary (**who** / **whom**) it considers excellent.

- Locate the noun clause in each sentence below.
- Mentally rearrange each noun clause into natural order where necessary to determine the function of the needed pronoun.
- Write the sentence inserting the correct pronoun.
- Label the principal parts of the main clause.

1. a. (**Who** / **Whom**) wins will depend on several factors.

    b. (**Who** / **Whom**) the judges select will depend on several factors.

   c. (**Who** / **Whom**) the winner will be will depend on several factors.

2. **a.** The question was (**who** / **whom**) had sent the package.

   b. The question was (**who** / **whom**) had the anonymous caller been.

   c. The question was (**who** / **whom**) had the maid told.

3. **a.** The police do not know (**who** / **whom**) the murderer is.

   b. They do not know (**who** / **whom**) called them.

   c. They do not know (**who** / **whom**) the assassin will kill next.

4. **a.** The prize goes to (**whoever** / **whomever**) sells the most subscriptions.

   b. The scholarship goes to (**whoever** / **whomever**) the board finds most deserving.

   c. A thanks goes to (**whoever** / **whomever**) our secret benefactors are.

G

- Number your paper from 1 to 12.
- Beside each number, write the function of the pronoun needed to complete the corresponding sentence below.
- After the stated function, write the correct pronoun.

1. This corsage is for (**who** / **whom**)?

2. Your escort can be (**whoever** / **whomever**) you choose.

3. The President (**who** / **whom**) promised to reduce taxes has tried to do so.

4. (**Who** / **Whom**) is the club supporting?

5. She loved (**whoever** / **whomever**) society had rejected.

6. (**Who** / **Whom**) washed the cars?

7. Most new assembly line workers (**who** / **whom**) the company has employed through your agency have proven themselves competent.

8. He is the man (**who** / **whom**) can lead our nation through this economic crisis.

9. (**Who** / **Whom**) the chaperones will be is your decision.

10. (**Who** / **Whom**) could the murderer have been?

11. His daughter was the one for (**who** / **whom**) the doctors held little hope.

12. I met the actor's mother (**who** / **whom**) the book had mentioned.

■ On your paper list the numbers of those sentences that need internal punctuation.

■ Beside each number, write the word(s) in the sentence that should be followed by a mark of punctuation.

SKILL TEST

■ Number your paper from 1 to 10.

■ Beside each number, write the function of the pronoun needed to complete the corresponding sentence below.

■ After the stated function, write the correct pronoun.

1. A small frail blonde child (**who** / **whom**) I had never seen before was following me.

2. To (**who** / **whom**) was the letter addressed?

3. This prize is for (**whoever** / **whomever**) sells ten tapes first.

4. (**Who** / **Whom**) have you discovered lately?

5. Do you know (**who** / **whom**) the manager of this store is?

6. Our neighbor (**who** / **whom**) has been having back problems is in the hospital.

7. (**Who** / **Whom**) brought the gift?

8. (**Who** / **Whom**) the administrators have approved for the position cannot be announced yet.

9. Mr. Walinski (**who** / **whom**) the board fired has been temporarily reinstated.

10. Betty likes (**who** / **whom**)?

■ On your paper list the numbers of those sentences that need internal punctuation.

■ Beside each write the word(s) in the sentence that should be followed by a mark of punctuation.

REVIEW A

■ On a separate sheet rewrite the sentences below correcting the pronoun errors.

1. Because my brother prepared well, it was easy for him to win.

2. Several on the list had mailed his payment.

3. The secretary who the agency sent was incompetent.

4. In his youth, Dad was a very good athlete.

5. The sophomores cleaned up the school grounds after their party, which pleased the administration.

6. Whom the woman was has remained a mystery.

7. The company has returned each of the checks to their owner.

8. Natalie often visited her sister when she was discouraged.

9. Who did you expect?

10. After he had left, Gary realized that the elderly man was his father's partner.

11. Neither the President nor her opponents had presented her arguments clearly.

12. Give the keys to whomever answers the door.

SKILL 4

Using Pronouns Correctly in Comparisons

In a comparison involving the use of the word *than* or *as,* a part of the sentence is often omitted. A <u>verb</u> is sometimes omitted to eliminate the repetition of a verb used earlier in the sentence. Note below.

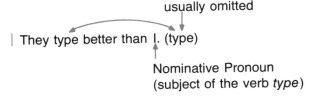

usually omitted

They type better than I. (type)

Nominative Pronoun
(subject of the verb *type*)

A grammatical error results when an <u>object pronoun</u> is used as the subject of an omitted verb. Study the examples below.

Wrong   You run as fast as him.

Correct   You run as fast as he. (runs)

(S)
n pro   AV

One can easily determine the correct pronoun form in comparisons by mentally inserting the usually omitted words. Note below.

?   ?
She left sooner than (**we** / **us**).

She left sooner than we. (left)

?   ?
Are you as excited as (**I** / **me**)?

Are you as excited as I? (am)

Usually words should not be omitted from a comparison involving three people or groups. When words are omitted in such comparisons, a sentence with an unclear meaning often results. Note the two possible meanings of the sentence that follows.

(Tim) teases (them) as much as (I / me).

Tim teases them as much as (he teases) me.

Tim teases them as much as I. (tease them)

CHECKUP

Answer the following questions on a separate sheet of paper.

1. What two words typically indicate comparisons?
2. What phenomenon usually occurs in sentences that involve the use of the words *than* and *as*.
3. How can the correct pronoun be determined in such sentences?
4. In what kinds of comparisons should words not be omitted?

A

On a separate sheet beside the corresponding number, write the pronoun found in the brackets that correctly completes the sentence.

1. I am as sorry about the incident as [**they** / **them**] (are).
2. The entire group seems as optimistic as [**she** / **her**] (seems).
3. She always studies more than [**us** / **we**] (do).
4. You are smarter than [**me** / **I**] (am).

283

B

■ On a separate sheet beside the corresponding number, write the pronoun found in the parentheses that correctly completes the sentence.

1. My opponent is taller and heavier than (**I** / **me**).

2. He cooks as well as (**her** / **she**).

3. Are all as qualified as (**them** / **they**)?

4. They are more involved in the plans than (**we** / **us**).

C

■ On a separate sheet write each sentence below.
■ Circle the three people or groups involved in each comparison.
■ Demonstrate the lack of clarity in the meaning of each sentence by writing the two interpretations of each, adding the usually omitted words.
■ Refer to the information designated by the symbol | | if you need help.

1. Mrs. Price likes her better than (**me** / **I**).

2. Did the manager offer you as much as (**they** / **them**)?

3. I trust him more than (**her** / **she**).

4. He should pay them as much as (**we** / **us**).

D

■ On a separate sheet beside the corresponding number, write the pronoun found in the parentheses that correctly completes the sentence.
■ If, however, a sentence involves a comparison that is unclear as written, write **incorrect** after the corresponding number.

1. Many admire her as much as (**he** / **him**).

2. I play tennis worse than (**her** / **she**).

3. You are more successful because you work harder then (**them** / **they**).

4. Are you as determined as (**us** / **we**)?

5. The boss should pay me as much as (**she** / **her**).

6. Chris likes Pam better than (**I** / **me**).

7. Others were as frightened as (**us** / **we**).

8. She gave them an easier test than (**me** / **I**).

9. On the slopes she was far better than (**he** / **him**).

10. We are as capable of winning as (**them** / **they**).

SKILL TEST

■ On a separate sheet beside the corresponding number, write the pronoun found in the parentheses that correctly completes the sentence.

■ If, however, a sentence involves a comparison that is unclear as written, write **incorrect** after the corresponding number.

1. Several others are being as difficult as (**they** / **them**).

2. I can understand him better than (**she** / **her**).

3. Tammy is more obstinate than (**he** / **him**).

4. The teacher appreciates you as much as (**I** / **me**).

5. Everyone is as excited about it as (**she** / **her**).

6. He gave you a better price than (**we** / **us**).

7. Did the company pay her as much as (**he** / **him**)?

8. Are you as hungry as (**I** / **me**)?

9. They are much younger than (**we** / **us**).

10. I do not type as fast as (**they** / **them**).

REVIEW A

■ Number your paper from 1 to 10.

■ If the sentence contains no pronoun error, write **C** beside the corresponding number.

■ Rewrite those sentences containing errors, correcting the pronoun problems.

1. After they had finished the table decorations, the caterers left for about an hour.

2. The committee chose chicken rather than steak because it was expensive.

3. My older brother is a better athlete than me.

4. Both Gail Washington and Nancy Rosenbloom made her appearance but left quickly.

5. Whom can the stranger be?

6. Everybody should choose a good hobby for himself.

7. Do you know whom the group will nominate?

8. In today's newscast, they said that the summit meeting is considered a success.

9. Jill saw Susan sitting near her father.

10. Neither taxes nor inflation will receive its deserved attention in this legislature.

REVIEW B

■ Number your paper from 1 to 10.
■ If the sentence contains no pronoun error, write **C** beside the corresponding number.
■ Rewrite those sentences containing errors, correcting the pronoun problems.

1. Whoever the group decides on for convention delegate will be fine with me.

2. Don't put the clay flowerpot on the antique marble-topped table until it is dry.

3. Both of the suggestions had its merits.

4. When Mother leaves my little sister at the nursery, she always cries.

5. I am looking for a reliable and conscientious babysitter whom my children will like.

6. Neither the committee members nor the chairman would say how they planned to vote on the issue.

7. In London you have to wear a raincoat almost every day.

8. Are all as well trained as him?

9. One of the students left her lunch on the bus.

10. Because of his operation, Mr. Myer was unable to attend his convention.

REVIEW C

■ Answer the following questions on a separate sheet of paper.

1. In a sentence how many commas are needed to separate three items in a series? Four items?

2. How does one punctuate a compound sentence in which the two main clauses are joined by a conjunction?

3. When is a comma before a conjunction connecting two main clauses unnecessary?

4. How is a sentence containing a series of short main clauses punctuated?

5. How does one punctuate a compound sentence in which the main clauses are joined by a conjunctive adverb?

6. Under what circumstances can a semicolon *alone* be used to separate the clauses of a compound sentence?

7. When is a semicolon, instead of a comma, placed before a conjunction connecting the main clauses of a compound sentence?

8. What are the five circumstances in which participial phrases are usually separated from the rest of the sentence by commas?

9. What are the four circumstances in which adjective clauses are usually separated from the main clause by commas?

10. Which adjective structure is always separated from the rest of the sentence by commas?

11. When are phrases and clauses used as adverbs separated from the rest of the sentence by commas?

REVIEW D

■ Write the sentences below skipping a line between each.
■ Underline the verb or verb phrase in each main clause.
■ Draw a bracket above any phrase or clause used as a noun; label appropriately.
■ Draw a broken line beneath any phrase or clause used as an adjective; label and draw an arrow to the word modified.
■ Draw a double line beneath any phrase or clause used as an adverb; label and draw an arrow to the word modified.
■ Label all other words.
■ Punctuate where necessary. On the line below each sentence explain your use of each internal mark of punctuation.

a. 1. Flagstaff located a hundred and twenty miles north of Phoenix is a refreshing retreat for Phoenicians.

2. The problems on the geometry exam seemed easy but I'm not sure that I did them correctly.

3. To secure a loan I made my father the promise that I would be more conscientious in my studies.

4. What you have done for us has made the difference between success and failure we wish to express publicly our heartfelt thanks.

5. The boss found the stranger a fast conscientious congenial worker who had considerable expertise.

6. The antique clock a gift from a favorite aunt was the possession that I valued most however my parents struggling to feed a large family during the recession were forced into a decision to sell it.

7. Keeping it a secret will be difficult to do this time.

8. I wrote it he typed it and she delivered it.

9. The irony of the situation was that the opponent was her brother.

10. Starving for both food and freedom many people from many countries migrated to this land of opportunity to search out a better life.

b. 1. If Andrew doesn't attend this practice he won't play in the next game unless we are short on substitutes.

2. The clock stopped so we were late.

3. The crystal and other fragile items that were of considerable value were packed with care by the movers but taking this precaution did not prevent our losing many items.

4. My brother Robert is in the Marines.

5. To leave then would have caused a disturbance consequently we determined to stay until the intermission.

6. After the concert on Thursday night I was too tired to go to the dance.

7. Our mayor acting on the suggestion of the city council made the retiring police chief an honorary member of the police department.

8. The improvements will depend on how much money we raise by that time.

9. Her favorite spot to campout was a small valley nestled in the White Mountains it was the subject of many of these sketches that are on display.

10. My greatest adventure was rearing my children.

c. 1. That small craft painted blue and white which is tied to the big boat was in the final race.

2. Although I'm an amateur I love skiing with my more experienced friends.

3. To arrive late is to miss the best part of the show so we should be ready to leave by seven.

4. My grandmother left me this lovely old marble-topped table which had been a gift to her from her own grandmother.

5. Procrastination will make our success impossible the time to act is now.

6. They left with Janice to pick up the doughnuts and cider as soon as they finished the door decorations.

7. Leaving the library I slipped on a pebble twisting my ankle badly.

8. She is counting on getting this job however I know that her chances are slim.

9. To avoid hitting the child he swerved his car a beautiful new Toyota off the road into a cement ditch.

10. After a brief discussion the committee hired Pat Holt who comes to us with excellent recommendations.

APPENDIX

Capitalization

A *proper noun,* a name of a specific person, place, or thing, should be capitalized.

When a proper noun consists of more than one word, the first letter of the first word and all important words are capitalized. (Short prepositions and the adjectives *a, an,* and *the* found between the first and last word are not capitalized.)

SPECIFIC PEOPLE

Friends
Jim, Marie, Cookie, Mort, Fonz, Arnold Schwartz, April Crowe

Relatives
Aunt Vera, Grandpa Jones, her cousin Alison, his wife Judy
What's for supper, Ⓜom?   My ⓜom is neat!

Acquaintances
Mr. and Mrs. Joseph Solano, Ms. Claudette Lutz, Dr. Loretta Stanley, Professor Sage, Lieutenant Eagleston

Prominant People
the President of the United States, the Queen of England, Representative John Deconcini, House Speaker Rayburn
a Ⓢenator from Washington
the Ⓢenator from Washington

SPECIFIC PLACES

Streets and Roads
Cactus Avenue, Fifty-second Street, Black Canyon Freeway, Interstate 17

Buildings
Empire State Building, Carnegie Hall, the Astrodome, the Capri Theater, the Dallas Public Library, Bellevue General Hospital, Museum of Modern Art

Schools
Glenview Elementary, Thunderbird High School, United States Air Force Academy

Amusement Parks	Encanto Park, Turf Paradise, Disney World, Golf'n Stuff
Cities and Counties	New Orleans, Kansas City, Dade County, Jefferson Parish
States and Sections of the Country	Cornbelt, Colorado, the Klondike, the Midwest, the Texas Panhandle, the Ohio Valley I drove Ⓢouth. I drove through the Ⓢouth.
Bodies of Water	Indian Ocean, Mississippi River, Gulf of Mexico, Lake Pontchartrain, Honey Island Swamp
Mountains	Camelback Mountain, Pike's Peak, Mount Rushmore, the Great Divide
Islands	Easter Island, the Isle of Mann a Hawaiian Ⓘsland the Hawaiian Ⓘslands
Countries and Continents	Brazil, Europe, Central America, Iran, North America, Antarctica, Puerto Rico
Planets and Constellations	Mars, Saturn, the North Star, Orion, the Big Dipper

SPECIFIC THINGS

Calendar Items and Specific Events	Monday, February, the Fourth of July, Thanksgiving, Ground Hog Day, Education Week, Texas State Fair, Southwestern Livestock Show, the Colonial Invitational
Historical Divisions of Time	the Atomic Age, the Elizabethan Period, the Kennedy Era, the Dark Ages
Historical Events	World War II, the London Blitz, the Constitutional Convention of 1787, the Great Depression
Historical Documents	the Declaration of Independence, the Fifth Amendment, the Emancipation Proclamation, the Magna Carta
Historical Treaties and Agreements	the Strategic Arms Limitation Treaty, the Middle East Accords, the North Atlantic Pact
Organizations	National Education Association, American Heart Institute, Salvation Army, Detroit Chamber of Commerce
Awards	the Presidential Scholarship, the Outstanding Athlete Award, the Nobel Peace Prize, the Congressional Medal of Honor

Art Objects	The *Mona Lisa, Portrait of a Young Woman, Moses, The Thinker*
Monuments	the Washington Monument, the Lincoln Memorial, the Statue of Liberty
Books and Chapters	*Gone with the Wind,* the *Bible, Genesis, The Fellowship of the Ring* Chapter 2, "The Northwest Exploration"
Periodicals and Articles	the *Reader's Digest, Cosmopolitan, The New York Times* "Sophomore Reading Scores Improve"
Plays and Movies	*The Taming of the Shrew, Dracula, Romeo and Juliet, Superman, Star Wars, Annie*
Short Stories and Poems	"The Gift of the Magi," "Stopping by Woods on a Snowy Evening"
Television Programs	"Mork and Mindy," "The Osmond Family Show," "Little House on the Prairie," "Battlestar Gallactica"
Musical Compositions	"My Favorite Things," "The Flight of the Bumble Bee," *Aida,* the *Grand Canyon Suite*
Courses	Algebra II, French, Drama 3–4, Communications and Mass Media, Family Living
Business Firms	Sperry Rand Corporation, Bell Telephone Company, Robinson's Jewelers, Burger King, National Textbook Company
Brand Names	a Chevrolet, a Ford pickup, Dial soap, Sears appliances, Dorito corn chips

PUNCTUATION

An exclamation point should follow a sentence that expresses strong feeling.

Quit!
It's gorgeous!
Bring the fire extinquisher!

A period follows an abbreviation.

Mr. J. M. Firestone   (Mister, John, Merrell)

Dr. Valeria Lima   (Doctor)

Lt. Carl Helms   (Lieutenant)

1427 Monument Blvd.   (Boulevard)

New Orleans, La.   (Louisiana)

A comma is used to separate two adjectives when a pause between them improves the readibility of the sentence.

He needed a long winter's nap.
He hated the long, involved discussion.

She was a pretty little girl.
She was a pretty, talented actress.

A colon is placed before a list of items introduced by expressions like *the following* and *as follows*.

The eligible students are the following: Cassandra Simon, Debbie Bunt, John Cohn, and David Meyer.

A colon should never separate a verb from its complement.

Wrong   The only ingredients are: chocolate chips, egg whites, and sugar.

Right   Three ingredients are necessary: chocolate chips, egg whites, and sugar.

A colon is used between the hour and the minutes when one is writing the time.

  5:30 a.m.   1:45 p.m.

A colon is used after the salutation of a business letter.

  Dear Sir:
  Dear Dr. Horton:
  Dear Madam:

QUOTATION MARKS

Quotation marks are used to set off a person's exact words.

In a <u>phrase</u>

He called me a "low-down polecat."

In a <u>statement</u>

Debbie announced, "I won't be here tomorrow."
"I won't be here tomorrow," Debbie announced.

In a <u>question</u>

Mr. Hudson asked, "What time is it?"
"What time is it?" asked Mr. Hudson.

In a <u>split statement</u>

Mrs. Kenny said, "He knows that the flight leaves at noon."
"He knows the flight leaves at noon," said Mrs. Kenny.
"He knows," said Mrs. Kenny, "that the flight leaves at noon."

Two sentences can be contained within one set of *quotation marks*.

Mr. Lewis said, "Study this article carefully. We'll discuss its major points tomorrow."

"Study this article carefully. We'll discuss its major points tomorrow," said Mr. Lewis.

"Study this article carefully," said Mr. Lewis. "We'll discuss its major points tomorrow."

Avoiding Double Negatives

Negatives are a small group of words used to express denials, contradictions, or opposites. Common negatives are the following:

no   hardly
not   scarcely
none
never
no one
nobody
nothing

Study the use of the negatives circled below.

Positive You broke the vase.
Negative I did (not) break the vase.

Positive He had some.
Negative He had (none).

Positive She asks questions.
Negative She (never) asks questions.

Only one negative is necessary to change a positive statement to a negative one. When two negatives are used, the result is a grammatical error called the *double negative.* Study the examples below.

Wrong   I have n't nothing to regret.
Right   I have nothing to regret.

Wrong   There was n't hardly time to finish.
Right   There was hardly time to finish.
Right   There was no time to finish.

Wrong   They do n't take no excuses.
Right   They do n't take any excuses.
                or
Right   They take no excuses.

Index

Index of Exercises and Drills

NTC LANGUAGE ARTS BOOKS

Business Communication
Handbook for Business Writing, *Baugh, Fryar, & Thomas*
Meetings: Rules & Procedures, *Pohl*

Dictionaries
British/American Language Dictionary, *Moss*
NTC's Classical Dictionary, *Room*
NTC's Dictionary of Changes in Meaning, *Room*
NTC's Dictionary of Debate, *Hanson*
NTC's Dictionary of Literary Terms, *Morner & Rausch*
NTC's Dictionary of Theatre and Drama Terms, *Mobley*
NTC's Dictionary of Word Origins, *Room*
NTC's Spell It Right Dictionary, *Downing*
Robin Hyman's Dictionary of Quotations

Essential Skills
Building Real Life English Skills, *Starkey & Penn*
Developing Creative & Critical Thinking, *Boostrom*
English Survival Series, *Maggs*
Essential Life Skills, *Starkey & Penn*
Essentials of English Grammar, *Baugh*
Essentials of Reading and Writing English Series
Grammar for Use, *Hall*
Grammar Step-by-Step, *Pratt*
Guide to Better English Spelling, *Furness*
How to Be a Rapid Reader, *Redway*
How to Improve Your Study Skills, *Coman & Heavers*
How to Write Term Papers and Reports, *Baugh*
NTC Skill Builders
Reading by Doing, *Simmons & Palmer*
303 Dumb Spelling Mistakes, *Downing*
TIME: We the People, *ed. Schinke-Llano*
Vocabulary by Doing, *Beckert*

Genre Literature
Coming of Age, *Emra*
The Detective Story, *Schwartz*
The Short Story & You, *Simmons & Stern*
Sports in Literature, *Emra*
You and Science Fiction, *Hollister*

Journalism
Getting Started in Journalism, *Harkrider*
Journalism Today! *Ferguson & Patten*
Publishing the Literary Magazine, *Klaiman*
UPI Stylebook, *United Press International*

Language, Literature, and Composition
African American Literature, *Worley & Perry*
An Anthology for Young Writers, *Meredith*
The Art of Composition, *Meredith*
Creative Writing, *Mueller & Reynolds*
Handbook for Practical Letter Writing, *Baugh*
How to Write Term Papers and Reports, *Baugh*

In a New Land, *Grossman & Schur*
Literature by Doing, *Tchudi & Yesner*
Lively Writing, *Schrank*
Look, Think & Write, *Leavitt & Sohn*
NTC Shakespeare Series
NTC Vocabulary Builders
Poetry by Doing, *Osborn*
World Literature, *Rosenberg*
Write to the Point! *Morgan*
The Writer's Handbook, *Karls & Szymanski*
Writing by Doing, *Sohn & Enger*
Writing in Action, *Meredith*

Media Communication
Getting Started in Mass Media, *Beckert*
Photography in Focus, *Jacobs & Kokrda*
Television Production Today!, *Bielak*
Understanding Mass Media, *Schrank*
Understanding the Film, *Bone & Johnson*

Mythology
The Ancient World, *Sawyer & Townsend*
Mythology and You, *Rosenberg & Baker*
Welcome to Ancient Greece, *Millard*
Welcome to Ancient Rome, *Millard*
World Mythology, *Rosenberg*

Speech
Activities for Effective Communication, *LiSacchi*
The Basics of Speech, *Galvin, Cooper, & Gordon*
Contemporary Speech, *HopKins & Whitaker*
Creative Speaking, *Frank*
Dynamics of Speech, *Myers & Herndon*
Getting Started in Oral Interpretation, *Naegelin & Krikac*
Getting Started in Public Speaking, *Carlin & Payne*
Listening by Doing, *Galvin*
Literature Alive, *Gamble & Gamble*
Person to Person, *Galvin & Book*
Public Speaking Today, *Carlin & Payne*
Speaking by Doing, *Buys, Sill, & Beck*

Theatre
Acting & Directing, *Grandstaff*
The Book of Cuttings for Acting & Directing, *Cassady*
The Book of Monologues for Aspiring Actors, *Cassady*
The Book of Scenes for Acting Practice, *Cassady*
The Book of Scenes for Aspiring Actors, *Cassady*
The Dynamics of Acting, *Snyder & Drumsta*
Getting Started in Theatre, *Pinnell*
An Introduction to Modern One-Act Plays, *Cassady*
An Introduction to Theatre and Drama, *Cassady & Cassady*
Play Production Today, *Beck et al.*
Stagecraft, *Beck*

For a current catalog and information about our complete line
of language arts books, write:
National Textbook Company
a division of NTC Publishing Group
4255 West Touhy Avenue
Lincolnwood (Chicago), Illinois 60646-1975 U.S.A.